DOORS OF PERCEPTION

A Guide to Reading the Psalms

PETER R. ACKROYD

Doors of Perception

A Guide to Reading the Psalms

SCM PRESS LTD

First published 1978
by The Faith Press

This edition published 1983
by SCM Press Ltd
26–30 Tottenham Road, London N1

Printed in Great Britain by
Richard Clay (The Chaucer Press) Ltd
Bungay, Suffolk

Contents

Foreword

Many who read *Doors of Perception* will be grateful to Professor Ackroyd for himself providing for them a door of perception into the meaning of the psalms. I certainly am grateful to him.

This is no detailed commentary on the psalms. It does not pretend to be. A much larger book would be needed for that (and a useful little bibliography is provided for those who wish to read more deeply). But the setting of the psalms in the wider context of psalm literature; the discussion of the nature and uses of poetry; the outline of the structures of verse which the psalmists use; and the exposition of certain psalms particularly in the last two chapters of the book—all these things put within our reach a key which will unlock much of the meaning of the psalms.

All churchmen use the psalms but all too few with the understanding which the psalms deserve. This book will increase the number of those who, like St. Paul, are intent on 'singing with the understanding also' (1 Cor. 14 : 15).

DONALD CANTUAR:

Preface

I WISH TO express my gratitude to Mr. Ivor Bulmer-Thomas whose original suggestion it was that I should write this book; and to the Archbishop of Canterbury and the Faith Press for accepting it as the Lent Book for 1978.

Books have a degree of independence, in that in some measure they write themselves, the pressures of the subject moving the author in directions which were not necessarily fully anticipated at the outset. I am deeply indebted to friends and colleagues, for the kindliness of encouragement and the stimulus of discussion of issues which appear here.

The title, *Doors of Perception*, I owe to Fr Harry Williams who used the phrase in his sensitive discussion *Tensions* (1976, p. 101), but he has pointed out to me that he in his turn took it from Aldous Huxley's book published under this title (*The Doors of Perception*, 1954).

References in the text by chapter and verse only, with no biblical book indicated, are always to the psalms. Where appropriate, the normal abbreviations for modern translations have been employed.

1

Of Literature and Life

I PRIDE MYSELF on being a 'Janeite'; the novels of Jane
Austen to which I return again and again and which I have
read aloud at least six times in their entirety are so familiar
that their detail is fixed in my mind. To be asked, as I was
recently, in relation to *Pride and Prejudice*: 'Who dressed
what and where?' could be answered, with no more than a
few moments of reflection: 'Lydia and Kitty, a sallad and
cucumber, at the inn when they met their sisters returning
from London'. There is nothing of merit in this, only a
delight in familiar words and familiar situations, and a continuing growth in appreciation of the skill of the writer. For
many years I read only the novels, but some ten years ago
I picked up a volume of essays on Jane Austen and read
them in small doses on my train journeys to the centre of
London. I do not know whether the particular author of
those essays ranks as an expert among those who know;
what I experienced was an even deeper pleasure in the novels
as I re-read them yet again. What Harry Williams calls 'doors
of perception' were opened. The change came from a greater
sensitivity, aroused by new information and suggestive questions; what spoke to me now was what had always been
there, but it was to be seen now with new eyes.

There is a danger in too much mere information. If we
look at a picture or read a poem or hear a piece of music
with our minds already conditioned by having been told what
it means, or how it is constructed, or whether its creator is

recognized as a good artist, a skilful poet, a musician of originality, then we may discover only what we have been told we ought to think. Fashions in appreciation are part of a complex process by which at a given moment particular styles of architecture or of furniture and house decoration are in vogue. Suddenly, as we have observed over recent years, Victoriana are no longer to be scoffed at, but regarded as worth collecting. Immediacy of contact with a work of art is the better starting-point, though such immediacy may both attract and repel. The picture may shock by the harshness of its colours; the music may seem to have nothing but inconsequence in its arrangement of sounds; the poem to be mere words. A second view, a second hearing, may evoke something further. It is when we have gone thus far that we may usefully turn to what we may learn from the creative artist himself, from those who are knowledgeable in the particular field, by way of enlarging our understanding, informing our minds, but most of all opening those 'doors of perception' by which we may be able to see more clearly for ourselves what has been there all the time.

The technique here is to read or to look or to hear first; to study and gain in understanding second; and then to go back for a renewed reading, a further hearing, another and closer look. And the process is capable, with a truly creative work, of indefinite repetition.

It was the author of Ecclesiastes who wrote: 'Of the making of many books there is no end' (12 : 12); and had he known how over the next 2,000 years there would be even more clearly no end to the making of books about the Bible (including many about his own endeavours at exploring the meaning of life), he might well have felt even greater depression. Much will be lost if the effect of such books is to take us away from what our religious tradition sets so centrally to the understanding and nourishment of faith. If the reading of books about the Bible—this one included—distracts us from the actual reading of the text, then it has failed in its prime task. If such reading takes us back to the text, with our eyes a little wider open, our minds a little more sensitive, then it will have achieved success. Ideally each reading of the text, and each reading of a guide to some aspect of its nature and interpretation, should open up for us more of what is there to be discovered.

For many, the reading of the psalms is made more difficult by familiarity; the older practices, still maintained in some places, of the reading or singing of the psalms in sequence through the daily services of a single calendar month, and in some contexts even more frequently repeated, have largely given way to more selective use, with shorter passages spread over a longer cycle. There may be gain as well as loss in such a change. A disadvantage, common to many traditions, is that psalms are only sung or said according to a particular pattern of reading, their verses divided into ungainly halves or read alternately by celebrant and congregation. Or they are sung in the skilled but often tortuous metrical forms associated with Scotland or in the paraphrased poetry of the hymn books, some good, some indifferent, and some indisputably bad. They are much less often read to be heard, like the poetry of prophets and of wisdom writers such as the author of Job, in a more continuous form. There is loss here too, since there is value in the reading of poetry aloud, with sensitivity and awareness of the movement of thought, which can easily be lost in the rigid forms of chant and equally in the freer but still stylised settings of Gelineau and the like.

We shall need to read for ourselves, and study and read again; we shall need also to encourage more experiment in the reading aloud of the poetry of the psalms which has established itself in its own right as poetry and is worth the hearing for that. Since poetry is a medium of communication from the mind of the writer to that of the reader, a mode of communication which seeks through its particular forms to express what cannot be so well presented in other styles of language or by other means, it is vital that we should be able to make contact, through the poetry, with the mind behind it, with the context from which it comes, and thereby enter

13

a new realm of experience and thought.

But there lies also much of our difficulty. We may discover the poetry of a writer unknown to us before, as not long ago I discovered that of Emily Dickinson. We may dip into the poems and find some of them odd and others rather curiously naive and yet others strangely moving; and all this without knowing anything more than perhaps has appeared from a very quick glance at the preface which informs us that she was American and nineteenth century. We may then hear, by chance, a broadcast programme in which the reading of her poems is interspersed with information about her relatively uneventful life, about her particular background of thought, and, as has already been suggested, come back to the poetry with a new awareness. For the psalms, the problems are different. We do not know the authors, nor can we hope by any amount of research to discover them, know their names, when they lived, how they came to write; indeed, for the psalms these may in some degree be the wrong questions to ask. In addition, they were written in Hebrew and their texts were transmitted, copied and recopied, over many centuries before the form in which we know them in that language became fully fixed. Translating poetry from one language to another is a delicate matter, requiring intimate knowledge of the original language and a real poetic sense in the handling of the language into which the translation is made. The ancient Hebrew language is still imperfectly known and discoveries continue to be made which illuminate uncertainties or modify accepted views. Something is said at the end of this book about translations and how they may be used (pp. 92-3). Here we may simply observe that the language and the text present one of the barriers to a full understanding and appreciation.

Furthermore, these are poems which belong to an ancient world, to a culture different from our own, even though our western culture has been deeply influenced by ideas and forms which derive from ancient Israel. The reading of the biblical writings introduces us to this different world, with its particular social structures, its ways of thought and behaviour. New discoveries shed light on the nature of that world; archaeology uncovers buildings and objects in daily use, so that we can form a clearer picture of how people lived. Aspects of political and social and economic life are disclosed. But much remains tentative, and the personalities, even where their names are well known, remain shadowy, their life-story impossible to reconstruct, the full entry into their experience and their thinking unavailable to us. Most of what we may say about the psalmists can only be derived from the reading of the poems themselves, since nowhere are we given any description of how psalms came to be written, and the few notes attached to them which associate them with particular persons or with particular situations are clearly to be seen as part of the process by which they have come to be interpreted, already within the formation of the biblical text.

This is all rather negative. What can we say more positively about their origin? Some aspects of this will become clearer in the course of this book, but we may start with the recognition that psalmody in Israel is not isolated in the ancient world. There are Babylonian and Egyptian psalms which are of the same kind of religious poetry as those which are familiar to us from the Bible. We do not as yet possess any Canaanite psalms as such, but we have much poetry which shows analogies with the psalms, similarities of language and style and metaphor. It is clear that Israel's psalms derive from a common heritage of religious poetry and cannot be fully understood without the recognition of the wider culture within which Israel itself developed.

It is also clear that such religious poetry cannot be tied down to particular periods or to particular persons as authors. To a very large extent—how far is a matter of discussion— the psalms are associated with worship; they belong to the great public celebrations; some of them may belong to more personal occasions, though here again there are uncertainties and difficulties of interpretation. There is, however, clear evidence that in the course of time, even if psalms originally belonged to the public occasion, they came to be seen as applicable to the needs of individual worshippers. Over the course of the period of roughly a thousand years—or more if we go farther back still—from the time of Israel's main settlement in Canaan to the point at which the last Old Testament writings were produced, the changes in the community's life, politically and socially and intellectually, were very great. If, as we may suppose, Israel already had religious poetry from the earliest times, then over the years this poetry must have been re-interpreted and in some measure re-shaped, to meet the needs and to correspond to the ways of thought which belonged to her changing conditions.

One notable moment in this can be particularly clearly detected, though not described in detail. The establishment of the Davidic dynasty was associated with the capture of Jerusalem and the building of a new shrine there, the Solomonic temple of Jerusalem, which was closely associated with the life and well-being of the kingdom. We may not improperly suppose that older religious poetry was in some measure updated at this point and that some strong influences were at work from the existing practices of the land whose culture and holy places Israel so substantially shared and adopted. Even though it is clear that pictures of David as the organiser of every detail of the temple worship—found especially in 1 Chronicles 15-29—must be regarded as a reflection of later ideas, it is evident that a new stage of religious development begins at this point. Whatever religious poetry Israel already possessed now came under the influence of a changed political and religious order. If it continued to be used, as may most naturally be assumed, it must have been at the very least re-interpreted, and probably in some measure modified. In addition, we need to ask what influence was exerted upon the development of Israel's religious poetry, as upon every aspect of her thinking, by the absorption into her life of the important Canaanite city-state of Jerusalem, now to be designated the city of David. How far did the new political order, supported as it very properly felt itself to be by religious sanctions, take over the religious poetry and other religious institutions of the political set-up which it replaced? May we detect, as some scholars believe we may, the presence of Canaanite psalms behind those which we know, psalms which were transformed by coming to be used in reference to Israel's God and his actions and nature? And what happened at this crucial moment may have its counterparts at other greater or lesser turning points of Israel's life, not least that of the experience of disaster and of exile in Babylon for many of the people in the sixth century B.C.

Detecting the degree to which this happened and the precise effects on the actual wording is difficult; there is a strong strain of conservatism in all religious life, a strong urge to preserve ancient ways and ancient traditions and familiar words. So poetry which belongs to an early date may continue to be used, though now very differently read and interpreted in a much later situation. One simple and very obvious example may be mentioned here, related to the point just made; it is one that touches on many of the problems of interpretation of the psalms. From about 1000 B.C., Israel was a monarchy. For roughly four hundred years, Judah had a king. The northern kingdom of Israel, separated from Judah after the death of Solomon, lost its monarchy roughly a century earlier. Not surprisingly, a number of psalms refer directly to the king (e.g. 45, 72). It is very probable that psalms without such direct reference also contain allusions to the king who appears as an important figure in Israel's worship. Solomon in 1 Kings 8 leads the celebration of the dedication of the new temple and this may be seen as an indication of regular royal function rather than as an isolated instance. Many scholars believe, and probably rightly, that much psalmody is linked to the position and function of the king as leader of the people and as claiming a particular relationship to God. In 587 B.C., Babylonian conquest brought about the end of the Davidic monarchy. For more than three centuries there was no king. When a new monarchy was established, described as such with the accession to power

17

B

of one of the Maccabaean family named Aristobulus who took the title of king in 104 B.C., the dynasty, known as the Hasmonean dynasty from the name of a remoter ancestor, was not universally acceptable and was short-lived, brought to an end with the intervention of Roman power in Palestine in the middle of the first century B.C.

Now during the long period when there was no king as political and religious leader, worship continued with the use of psalms which made clear or implicit reference to the king. For this to be possible, re-interpretation must have taken place. It is possible that in some instances the older wording was changed, but even without any changes the older forms could be re-applied, understood as relevant to contemporary needs. In fact this same point can be made in regard to virtually all the Old Testament writings. The words of the prophets were handed down and seen to have meaning for new situations; they were collected and re-shaped in the process of interpretation. And the same applies to stories and laws and other forms of the literature. What is more, we may see that this process, already very clearly traceable within the pages of the Bible itself, went on continuously even when the biblical text had come to be fixed as unalterable. Commentaries and paraphrases by Jewish teachers, re-interpretations by early Christian writers and by commentators down the centuries, continued to make the point that the religious value and significance of the psalms were not to be limited merely to attempts at discovering what men thought and believed when the psalms were first composed and used. It was possible to see them as meaningful for each new generation, and to derive a deeper understanding of the meaning of faith and a fuller sense of what is meant by the experience of God, by the exploration of what the ancient poets and their earliest interpreters had set out.

This is not a process in which we can simply call a halt at a certain moment in time and say that finality has been reached. We may very properly continue to press on with the task of discovering the meanings of words, the religious prac-

18

tices and beliefs which underlie the psalms, and so endeavour to reconstruct the earliest stages to which we can reach. But we are not dealing here with a mere matter of historical reconstruction; we are dealing with questions of belief, of apprehension of God and his nature, of the ways in which these things can be expressed in the limiting language at our disposal. A great poem—religious or not—is one which expresses the insights, the experiences and emotions, the sensitivity and the suffering, of the poet who wrote it. We may search out the occasion of its writing, explore the circumstances and conditions in which its writer was at work, assess the relationship between literature and life to be seen there. And, of course we could, if we wished, stop there. But the poet and his poetry do not stop there; he continues to speak, whether we listen or not. He speaks across the years and across from one culture to another, out of the depth of human experience. He may speak of love and evoke in us, the readers, generations away, a new perception of what love is; the Song of Songs can speak to us of that, as plainly as e. e. cummings or Jon Stallworthy. He may speak of death and the brevity of human life; and he may be the author of the book of Job or John Betjeman or Stevie Smith. He may speak of God and of man, of creation and eternity, of good and evil and of the mysteries of human experience; and he may be speaking through a familiar psalm or in the sonnets of John Donne or the songs of Sydney Carter.

Not all of these will speak to all of us at any one moment. Not all the psalms will speak to us at a given time, though as we come back to them again and again, we shall find that new insights open up. Some of them will remain silent for us, while they speak to our friends. Some of them will be always alive for us, a source of increasing penetration into the greatest mysteries of our human experience. It is for us to let them speak, enabling their speech to be heard by our willingness to become more sensitive, but not supposing that we must force out a meaning against their will. For if we try to do that, making them all fit the pattern of our own think-

19

ing, compelling them all to confirm what we believe, we shall merely have imposed on them something which does not belong, and we shall have missed their deeper insights and the questions which they pose, often to cherished ideas and favourite misconceptions.

Through Literature to Life was the title of a book by Ernest Raymond; it speaks of the discovery of the richness of experience in the exploration of literature. We must not claim too much for the psalms, nor expect everything to follow from our reading and our study; but we should be depriving ourselves of a rich spring of religious understanding, a whole realm of religious life and experience, if we cut ourselves off from this relatively small but incomparably moving collection of poetry.

2

Psalms and Canticles

THE REGULAR USE of the psalms in worship covers the 150 poems in the Psalter. A glance at some Roman Catholic translations immediately shows a difference in numbering resulting from the fact that these are linked to the Vulgate (the standard Latin version of the Bible produced by Jerome about A.D. 400) and hence to the Septuagint (the Greek version). The total of 150 remains the same, but 9 and 10 are read as one psalm (and this is clearly right and is followed in newer translations too), and so the numbering differs by one from that point. Then 114 and 115 are read together as one (though this is less likely to be right); but 116 is divided into two separate psalms (which certainly makes good sense), and so the difference of one continues, until 147 is divided into two (again a convenient division), and the two forms of the Psalter end up with the same total.

It is convenient to know this, as we may find ourselves using a psalter numbered in an unfamiliar manner. But the point is more important for another reason. This will be clear if we observe some other facts. In a number of instances the same passages appear in more than one psalm: thus, in 108, verses 1-5 are the same as 57, verses 7-11; and verses 6-13 are the same as 60, verses 5-12. Thus it would appear that 108, like 116 just mentioned, could be treated as two separate units. On the other hand, it is evident that, perhaps for some liturgical purpose, separate passages could be joined, as when the Greek texts read 114 and 115 together.

21

Where in the Hebrew tradition, 9 and 10 were divided, it was evidently felt proper to use its two parts separately. There is a new start at 10 : 1—'Why, O God, do you stand far off?' —and we may sense a certain completeness in the content of 9 which is largely concerned with the supremacy and power of God over against the nations of the world. But it is entirely right that the Greek texts join these two psalms together; one clear reason for this is the presence in the Hebrew of an alphabetic acrostic—that is, the units of the poem, roughly corresponding to each two verses of the psalm, begin with the 22 successive letters of the Hebrew alphabet. The text is disordered at some points, but the acrostic extends through 9 and 10 together. Such alphabetic psalms are well known. In some cases, as in 145, each verse begins with a new letter; in others, a more elaborate pattern is followed. This may be seen in the first four chapters of Lamentations, a book which really consists of psalms of a particular kind, and most elaborately of all in 119 where each group of eight verses begins with the same letter. Some translations (e.g. A.V., R.V., and N.A.B.) mark this by putting the names of the letters—Aleph, Beth, Gimel, etc., at the head of each section. The Knox translation reproduces the pattern:

> Ah, blessed they, who pass through life's journey unstained, who follow the law of the Lord!
> Ah, blessed they, who cherish his decrees, make him the whole quest of their hearts!
> Afar from wrong doing, thy sure paths they tread.
> Above all else it binds us, the charge thou hast given us to keep (119 : 1-4).

But it is doubtful if such a poetic conceit can be transposed entirely satisfactorily into another language.

42 and 43 may also be seen to be parts of one psalm, though they are treated separately in both the Hebrew and the Greek. Their unity is marked by the appearance of a refrain in 42 : 5 and 11 and in 43 : 5, and another

22

refrain in parts of 42 : 9 and 43 : 2. Examination of the psalms
in detail suggests the possibility that yet others, not divided
in any of the texts, could be treated as consisting of more
than one unit. This may be true of 19, though there is an
interesting correspondence of thought here between the order
of creation in the first part (vv. 1-6) and the order of the life
of man obedient to God's law in the second (vv. 7-14).
27 has also been thought to consist of two quite separate
elements, different in content and style (vv. 1-6 and 7-14).
Our difficulty is that we cannot always be sure of the line of
thought which the poet is following; what may seem to us to
be unrelated could, for him, belong closely together.

It is, however, also quite clear that in ancient times different
elements of psalmody could be linked together, and this may
be true of other psalms in the Psalter. The uses of worship,
ancient and more modern, have probably had their influence
on the ways in which psalms are divided and joined. In some
cases we should perhaps describe a particular psalm as a
'liturgy' in that it takes the worshipper through the various
moments of invocation to God, confession of need, acknowledgement of God's power and action, recognition of his
willingness to respond to prayer, thanksgiving and rededica-
tion in renewed confidence. Such a pattern may be seen in
28: the psalmist calls urgently to God for help (vv. 1-2), he
asks that he, who thus turns to God, should not be treated
like evil men who behave deceitfully (vv. 3-4), and who do not
regard God's works (v. 5). In the conviction of God's answer,
he offers both an act of praise (v. 6) and a renewed confession
of faith (vv. 7-8). The psalm ends with an appeal, clearly
based on this liturgy, for the blessing of the people of God
(v. 9). The influence of worship on the combining of passages
of psalmody may also be observed in one of the few accounts
which we have of worship in biblical times.

In 1 Chron. 16, as part of the account of David bringing
the Ark to Jerusalem, a description is given of the ordering
of worship, here ascribed to David, and a psalm is quoted as
being that which was used on this the first occasion of public

23

worship under the new dispensation. When we look at the passage quoted, we observe that the first part (vv. 8-22) is the same as 105 : 1-15, and that the second part (vv. 23-33) is the same as 96 : 1-13. This account comes in a relatively late writing, possibly belonging to the fourth century B.C. and much later than the books of Samuel in which a different and indeed much simpler account is given of the bringing of the Ark to Jerusalem (2 Sam. 6). It is probable that the author of the later work, whose interest in David is an important clue to understanding how in the course of time a high value came to be set on his religious functions, thought it proper to elaborate the story. We may suspect that he was illustrating it here with a passage of psalmody familiar to him from the usage of his own time; perhaps he was in reality describing worship with the use of a psalm as he knew it. It is possible that he simply joined together two passages of psalmody, chosen because he felt them to be suitable to the occasion described; it is more probable that he is quoting a psalm as it was known to him and which, like 108, we can recognize as combining two elements. The usages of worship may thus result in the re-interpretation of already existing psalms, combining of separate elements, utilising of short extracts, and thus building up new psalms in the form in which we know them.

This account in 1 Chron. 16 provides another clue too. Following on the two psalm passages already noted, we have three concluding verses. Verse 34—'Praise God for he is good: his love is indeed for ever'—appears in a number of other places, e.g. 107 : 1; 136 : 1, and we may see an almost identical form of it, set in a similar context of worship, in 2 Chron. 20 : 21. Verse 35 corresponds to 106 : 47:

> Save us, O God of our victory,
>   gather us and deliver us from the nations,
> that we may praise your holy name
>   and boast of your praise.

Such an appeal to God to save Israel from the nations and

24

to gather the people together again is frequent at the end of a psalm: a similar sentiment, in quite different words, stands at the end of 14 = 53. Another small clue appears in 1 Chron. 16, for this verse 35 is introduced by the command: 'Say!' perhaps a summons to the assembly to join in a closing prayer, not really part of the preceding psalm. Verse 36 in 1 Chron. 16 is an ascription of praise to God:

> Blessed be the God of Israel
> for ever and ever.

It is the same as appears in 106 : 48, but it is not really part of that psalm; it is a doxology to one of the books into which the Psalter is divided.

In Hebrew tradition the Psalter was divided into five books (1-42; 43-72; 73-89; 90-106; 107-150), on the analogy of the first five books of the Bible, Genesis to Deuteronomy, which are known as the books of the Law. The Hebrew word for this—*Torah*—means law but is expressive of God's directives for his people's whole way of life. The association of the giving of the Israelite law with Moses led to these books being called the 'five books of Moses'; frequently in modern writings the Greek term Pentateuch—five scrolls—is used. The division of the Psalter into five books, linked to this, may be connected with liturgical use. At the end of each of the books of the Psalter there is a doxology, a blessing, with 150 doing duty at the end as a more elaborate one. The doxology in 1 Chron. 16 : 36 may best be seen as a concluding act of praise to the psalm just quoted. Thus it ends with a response, an appeal for deliverance, and an act of praise; and to this is added the comment: 'Then all the people said "Amen" and "Praise God"' and this provides another small clue to how worship was conducted. Was this perhaps a normal way of using the psalms in public worship, just as Christian practice has added the *Gloria;* and was it then used to conclude the separate books in the Psalter?

The effect of such an addition is to provide a new context for the words of the psalm. Such a final act of praise added

25

to a Hebrew psalm would mean that whatever the psalm says—by way of thanksgiving, of penitence, of appeal—is related to the acclamation of God as the eternal one to whom all praise is due. The Christian formula of the *Gloria* sets a psalm similarly in the context of such acclamation, affirming the nature of God as declared in Jesus as son of God and in the Holy Spirit as expressive of God's continuing activity. All the richness of Christian thought on God as he is understood in the threefold formula is here drawn together in one focus.

These points already begin to indicate something of the ways in which the psalms were used, and from them we go on to a further piece of evidence. This is the presence in various books of the Old Testament of a number of poems which are in effect psalms outside the Psalter. Some of these are traditionally collected together in biblical manuscripts as the 'odes' or 'canticles', together with such New Testament psalms as the *Magnificat* (Luke 1 : 46-55) and the *Benedictus* (Luke 1 : 68-79). Thus Exodus 15 : 1-21 is a psalm set in the story of Israel's crossing of the sea at the escape from Egypt. Deuteronomy 32 : 1-44 is one placed with other 'last words' of Moses, and reflects on the whole history of Israel and its meaning. 1 Samuel 2 : 1-10 is a prayer put into the mouth of Hannah at the dedication of the child Samuel to temple service. Isaiah 38 : 10-20 is a psalm ascribed to Hezekiah on his recovery from illness, and Jonah 2 : 2-9 one put into the mouth of the prophet when he is brought back to land by the great fish. Habakkuk 3 is a psalm, attached to the two preceding chapters of prophetic material; in this particular case, its designation as a psalm is made absolutely clear by the fact that it bears the same kind of heading and conclusion which may be found in the psalms of the Psalter: it reads

A prayer of Habakkuk the prophet: upon *shigionoth* (v. 1)

and

For the *menasseah* on my *neginoth* (v. 19b).

The curious terms which appear here are found, together with

26

various others, in the headings to the psalms in the Psalter. Along with them, as here, there sometimes appear completely intelligible phrases, and we shall see something of their significance later. The technical terms, left untranslated here because of the extreme difficulty of knowing with any degree of certainty what they mean, are probably to be seen as musical or liturgical expressions, like that other obscure word *Selah* which appears within the actual text of some psalms, often now omitted in translation. The Greek translators thought that *Selah* marked a division in the psalm, but if it was, we do not know whether this was the point for a response by the worshippers or for some music, such as a blast on a ram's horn. A technical term such as *menasseah* has been very variously explained: 'for the director', that is, the leader of worship, associated with the leadership in praise which in 1 Chron. 15-16 is ascribed to particular groups of Levites; or 'for propitiation', that is, to be associated with acts of worship in which the favour of God is sought and in particular the appeasement of divine disfavour; and these are only two possibilities which have been suggested. Fuller discussion of these terms would be inappropriate here; it may be found in some of the commentaries noted later (cf. p. 94).

The reading of the narrative books of the Old Testament reveals a number of such psalms; there are others to be found in the prophetic books, as we have just seen, but some of these are less easy to separate out than Hab. 3. It is not always clear how far such passages are to be regarded as psalms, though this is very likely for the poem quoted in Isaiah 12; or how far we may suppose that the prophets and those who interpreted them made use of psalm language and of the poetic structures found in the psalms for the expression of their thought. The prophecies of Isa. 40-55, often designated the words of the 'Second Isaiah', are shot through with language found in hymnic psalms; it would seem likely here that the prophet was offering an interpretation of his own time, the period of the Babylonian exile in the sixth century B.C., by showing the meaning of such hymnic language to the needs and aspirations of that period. This in itself shows something of the ways in which the rich store of religious poetry which we know in the psalms could be used for the expression of profound theological thinking.

There are two things which follow from this recognition of psalmody outside the Psalter. The first is the simple and obvious point that it adds to our knowledge of ancient Israel's psalm-poetry, providing us with a wider range of material to study and offering further examples of types of psalmody already known to us. It is like the discovery of a manuscript containing some unknown poems by a well-known writer. Another collection of such poems is known as the Psalms of Solomon; this appears in some of the important Greek manuscripts. Over recent years our knowledge of psalmody has in fact been even further extended by the discovery of the manuscripts from the Qumran area, often described as the Dead Sea Scrolls. One of these is a scroll of poems usually given the title of 'Hymns' or 'Hymns of Praise' because a number of them begin 'I will give thanks'. Estimates of their poetic value vary. They are rich in biblical allusion, which some commentators have thought reduce their claim to originality; but this very use of the biblical phraseology shows them to stand in succession to the psalms of the Psalter. A brief extract may serve to illustrate this.

> I thank thee, O Lord,
>> for thou has enlightened me through thy truth.
> In thy marvellous mysteries,
>> and in thy lovingkindness to a man [of vanity
>> and] in the greatness of thy mercy to a perverse heart
> Thou hast granted me knowledge.
>
> Who is like thee amoung the gods, O Lord,
>> and who is according to thy truth?
> Who, when he is judged,
>> shall be righteous before thee?

(Opening of hymn 12 from the translation by G. Vermes).

In addition to these psalms, various collections of poems have been found, one of which, the Psalms Scroll from Cave 11, contains not only numerous poems known to us from the Psalter though in a different order and in some instances with a somewhat different text, but also a number of poems not previously known in Hebrew. Two of these, indeed, appear in Greek texts as an addition to the Psalter, as a single poem associated by its title with David's killing of Goliath (1 Sam. 17); in the Hebrew it appears as two poems, the first a poetic version of the choosing of David the shepherd boy to be the leader of his people (1 Sam. 16), the second a fragment referring to the Philistine giant. Two others were known from Syriac translations, forming part of the Psalter in some Syriac-speaking churches. Yet others in this manuscript are previously unknown or only partially known poems, related to psalms and in some instances to the kind of writings found in books such as Proverbs and as Ecclesiasticus in the Apocrypha.

All this shows a wealth of poetry which provides a fuller context for our reading of the psalms in the Psalter. The fact that that collection stands apart should not allow us to forget the wider range.

The second point is the more important. The Psalter simply sets the psalms one after another. It is sometimes possible to suggest links between individual psalms—23 has been thought to provide an answer in the confidence of faith to the despair uttered in 22; the group of psalms 120-134— the Songs of Ascents (see p. 47)—show much interlinkage of thought and style. For the most part, conclusions regarding use and interpretation can only be based on the internal evidence of the texts themselves. But when we find a psalm set in a narrative, or acting as a conclusion to a collection of prophecies, we may at least detect something of the way in which these psalms were understood at one stage of their use.

In such cases, it is abundantly clear that the poems are being given a new interpretation. The poem which is set in 1 Sam. 2:1-10 as the prayer of Hannah clearly belongs originally to a different setting. Much of its allusion is to the king and to his position. We see here how a psalm which is primarily concerned with the position of the king in power and victory, acknowledging the supremacy of God and reflecting on the way in which the fortunes of men are at his disposal, has been used to provide a suitable prayer for a woman giving thanks for the gift of a son. We may recognize the probability that at a certain stage in the development of psalmody it was possible for such a reinterpretation to take place. What belongs to the king and to his exalted position under God, can be true also of the ordinary worshipper. At the same time we may observe that the insertion of the psalm here serves another function. It provides a broader comment on the significance of the birth of Samuel who was to be portrayed as responsible for the change over to the new political system of the monarchy, a change which was to have far-reaching religious consequences.

A similar point may be made about the psalm in Isa. 38. This chapter tells the story of King Hezekiah's illness and recovery, and it may be read in a different form in 2 Kings 20 : 1-11. One of the differences is the insertion of the psalm in the Isaiah form of the text. It purports to be the psalm of thanksgiving spoken by the king; in its form and style it is not inappropriate to such a situation, but we may doubt whether it originally belonged in this particular context. It appears to have a much wider reference than simply to illness. Here is a different case, one in which a psalm expressive of some general distress has been applied to a particular king, but with the added point that the story of Hezekiah's illness and recovery, together with the story that follows in Isa. 39 (2 Kings 20 : 12-19), is not really concerned simply with telling us about that particular moment in time. It is directed rather towards the distresses which came upon the whole community a century later, with the conquest of Judah by Babylon and the exiling of the leaders. The stories of Isa. 38-39 are told to bring hope and meaning to the lives of those who are in the distress of exile. Here is another kind of reapplication, one made to the needs of the community rather than to those of the individual.

When a psalm appears in a prophetic book, it may be seen to perform another kind of function. The psalm quoted in Isa. 12 provides a concluding comment to chapters 1-12. What follows is clearly quite separate. The whole complex collection in these opening chapters of the book shows the wider significance of what was said by Isaiah to Judah in the latter half of the eighth century (roughly 740 to 700 B.C.); the message is clearly here presented in a later situation, especially with reference to the time of Judah's total collapse in the sixth century. In that time of distress, the words of Isaiah have been re-interpreted to point to the significance of judgement and to the basis of hope in the saving power of God. This theme is particularly brought out in chapter 11, and chapter 12 offers a response in psalm form to the confidence of divine deliverance. In the psalm quoted here the first part (vv. 1-3) is noteworthy in that it uses three times the word for 'deliverance' or 'salvation' which is the basis of the prophet's name Isaiah ('God is victory, deliverance, salvation'). It would seem that whoever added this psalm wished the readers to recognize that the significance of this prophet's message, now looked at in a wider context, was to be seen in the very name which he bore. And it is worth recalling that the name Joshua, the same name as Jesus, expresses this same confidence in God's saving power. To this a further part is added (vv. 4-6), joining the whole community in an act of praise to the God who is both victor and present as the holy God in majesty in their midst. We may perhaps see similar functions being performed by the psalm which concludes the book of Habakkuk, and possibly by Micah 7 : 7-20 which may be regarded as a psalm. Another such comment, but here set before the prophetic words, is to be found in a psalm in the book of Nahum (1 : 2-11). Here the acclamation of the God who is supreme in victory over all his adversaries provides an interpretative context for the grim oracles of doom on the Assyrian capital of Nineveh set out in chapters 2 and 3. It is

31

an invitation to the reader to recognize that the downfall of the great imperial power, supreme for so long in the experience of Israel and Judah, is not to be seen merely as a historical event, but as a token of the supremacy of the God who brings all nations into subjection and by his power overcomes all that is set against his will

The placing of psalms in narrative and prophetic books thus serves a function in interpretation. The narratives or the groups of prophecies are to be seen in a new light, their wider significance drawn out. This is done, not by the addition of a sermon—though such a method is to be found for example in the sermon of Lev. 26 which interprets the preceding legal collections—but with a psalm which invites the reader to consider the theological meaning of the stories or prophecies he has been reading in the light of the particular points made in the psalm. At the same time, we may see that a psalm so set itself acquires a different meaning by being given a precise context of interpretation.

This is a point which becomes clear when we look at 18. This psalm appears twice: 18 in the Psalter, and 2 Sam. 22, as part of a concluding section (chapters 21-24) of the books of Samuel. When we read it in the Psalter, we have only the actual wording of the psalm as the basis for our interpretation of it—apart from one other element which will be mentioned in a moment. But in 2 Samuel it is given a context. Its relationship there with what precedes and follows invites the reader to understand the psalm in a particular manner, and also to understand the narratives with reference to the psalm. We may note that it is placed alongside another, otherwise unknown, psalm, 2 Sam. 23 : 1-7. This is described as 'the last words of David', a psalm which is concerned with the position ascribed to David as the divinely chosen ruler and as the founder of the dynasty, and issues more broadly in a reflection upon God's rule in justice and in the contrast between the blessings enjoyed by the loyal and the fate of those who pay no regard to the ways of God. As such it is a very fitting comment on the whole life and reign of David

in which the themes of loyalty and disobedience are interwoven with great skill. A similar placing together of two
psalms may also be seen in Deut. 32 and 33, and it seems
clear that the compiler of the whole continuous work from
Deuteronomy to 2 Kings used this device first in regard to
the life and achievement of Moses and then to that of David.
These are the two figures—the great law-giver and founder
of Israel's religious life, and the great king and founder of
the dynasty—who can be seen to mark high points in the
narrative. Deut. 32, with its survey of Israel's experience and
its assessment of the community's relationship to God, provides a comment on the whole meaning of what happened
through the years from the exodus to the exile. 2 Sam. 22
expresses confidence in divine power and protection, it reflects on the ways of God with the faithful and the unfaithful;
and it assesses the place of the Davidic kings to whom God
gives victory and power. Thus it offers both an interpretation
of the period of the monarchy and affirms, as the whole of
the rather sorry story of that period is considered, that the
power of God to deliver remains constant, even in the times
of disaster and exile to which the community has eventually
come.

But we may note a further way in which interpretation is
offered. The heading of the psalm in both its occurrences
provides a clue to its interpretation at one stage of its use.
'David spoke to God the words of this song at the time when
God had delivered him from the power of all his enemies and
from the power of Saul'. This provides us with a link with a
theme used at some very important moments in the books of
Samuel. David's victories are acclaimed by the women of
Israel as greater than those of Saul, and Saul's comment is
given as 'What yet can be his but the kingship?' (1 Sam.
18 : 8). The bond between David and Jonathan involves the
recognition by Jonathan that true kingship will belong to
David, and he appeals to David for the continuing of that
loyal bond 'even when God cuts off from the ground each one
of David's enemies' (1 Sam. 20 : 15). The theme of continu-

33

C

ing victory marks many stories in the remainder of 1 Samuel and the opening chapters of 2 Samuel, until a climax is reached when 'God had given him rest all around from all his enemies' (2 Sam. 7 : 1), an echo of the opening of Deut. 12 and marking the moment for David to think of the building of a permanent shrine in Jerusalem, a task to be fulfilled by Solomon his successor. In the next chapter (2 Sam. 8), a summary is given of David's victories, and this is followed by a series of stories which tell of yet others—over the Ammonites (10-12), over his rebellious son Absalom (13-19), over another rebel, Sheba (20). So the psalm in 2 Sam. 22 invites the reader to look back over this whole story as a single unit.

The appearance of such a title to the psalm both in 2 Sam. 22 and in Ps. 18 gives us an example of one way in which psalms came to be understood in relation to the actual experience of David, and this is part of a process by which eventually it came to be believed that David was responsible for all the psalms. Something of the way in which this happened may be seen if we look at psalm titles which make such reference precisely. Thus 3 has a title: 'A psalm of David, when he fled from Absalom his son'. The psalm speaks of the many enemies of the psalmist, and of their mockery of his belief in divine help; it expresses confidence in divine protection and of God's answer to the prayer for help. It expresses assurance of divine watchfulness in the dangers of night-time, and the absence of fear which derives from that confidence. It culminates in a renewed appeal for divine action, expressing the assurance that God is victor; and invites the acknowledgement that 'deliverance rests with God', asking God's blessing upon the whole people. Nothing of this is really concerned with Absalom and his rebellion, and there is nowhere any direct allusion to the particular poignancy of the father-son relationship expressed in the stories in 2 Sam. 13-19. But the reader of the psalm is being invited to see in the story of David an example of experience from which he can learn to assess his own fears and anxieties. A psalm concerned with the divine protection of king and people and expressive of confidence in victory and blessing is taken through two stages of interpretation: it is to be read alongside the story of David and Absalom, and through that it is to become a vehicle for the religious needs and aspirations of the worshipping community and individual. Other psalms with such titles can be examined in the same way (see 7, 34, 51, 52, 54, 56, 57, 59, 60, 63 and 142); it may be noted that the precise reference to the story of David is not in every case completely clear. Other such references may also be found, particularly in later forms of the psalter; thus 80 has a heading in its Greek translation 'Concerning the Assyrian', which probably invites the reader to see it as a comment on the deliverance of king and people from the Assyrian invaders in the time of Hezekiah and Isaiah (cf. Kings 18-19; Isa. 36-37).

The association of psalms with the story of David may be traced a stage further. There is good reason to believe that spaces left in the ancient Hebrew manuscripts of 2 Samuel were in at least some instances designed to invite the reader to consider a relevant psalm at that point. In 2 Sam. 7 : 4 a space after the name Nathan provides a point to read 132; this describes the Ark of God as symbol of the divine power in relation to David's wish to build a temple, and links this to the divine promise to David of a lasting dynasty and to choice of Zion as God's holy dwelling. Similarly in 2 Sam. 12 : 13 at David's acknowledgement of his adultery with Bathsheba and his murder of Uriah, the reader is invited to read 51; and again at 2 Sam. 16 : 13, at the heart of the story of David's flight from Absalom, we are invited to read 3. Verse 3 of this psalm runs: 'There are many who say of me (literally: 'of my person' or 'my life'): How can there be salvation for him with God?' A Jewish commentary has: 'How can there be salvation for a man who had taken the lamb captive and slew the shepherd and who caused Israel to fall by the sword?' By this comment the theme of David and Bathsheba and Uriah and that of the judgement on David in Absalom's rebellion and its disasters for the whole people are drawn together; and the psalmist's confidence in God alone is aligned

35

with David's willingness to let the decision rest with God. As David says of Shimei who curses him (2 Sam. 16 : 11f.): 'If my son, my very own son, seeks my life, why should not this Benjaminite act thus. Let him alone, that he may curse if God has told him to do so. Maybe God will see my humiliation, and will requite me with good in the place of his curse today'. The psalmist's confidence, like David's, is in God alone.

Thus clues emerge to enable us to see something of the way in which psalms came to be interpreted. Our reading of them inevitably begins from a particular stage in this process of interpretation. This is true when we look, as we have been doing, largely at psalms outside the Psalter and at some clues within it, to see how they were applied to new situations or more particularly how they were used to point to a particular line of interpretation. It is also true when we look at the collection of psalms which makes up the particular book of 150 psalms which is familiar to us. We have noted that this collection is divided into five books on the analogy of the five books of Moses. From Jewish traditions we know something of the way in which these books were read in the synagogue, spread over either a three-year cycle of readings (divided into 154 sections to fit roughly the number of sabbaths), or over an annual cycle (divided into 53 or 54 sections). The former appears to have been a Palestinian system, the latter, which ultimately prevailed, developed among the Babylonian Jews. Just when these systems developed is not clearly known, but it has been thought that the total of 150 psalms was in some way related to a three-year system. It is, in any case, very likely that there is some link between the formation of the Psalter, including the actual ordering of the psalms in it, and the worship of the community. It is much less easy to discover exactly how and when this took place. Since the Psalms Scroll from Cave 11 at Qumran shows evidence of a different order and of different psalms, we may have some clue here to diversity of practice which was only gradually resolved completely, though the Greek translation probably shows that a Psalter virtually identical with the one we know must have been in existence during the last centuries B.C.

The detail of this is here less important than the recognition that there are indications of the way in which not only the psalms but all other parts of the Old Testament underwent a long process of exposition. This can be traced in the Qumran material, in the New Testament, and in much Jewish writing of the early centuries of the Christian era. Detailed study of the texts in fact points us back into the Old Testament period itself. Clues appear in the psalms, as in other Old Testament writings, of the ways in which earlier material was re-interpreted, applied to the needs of new situations. If we compare another pair of virtually identical psalms—14 and 53—clearly two copies of a psalm but with some marked differences—we get hints of the way in which the differences point to two stages of application of the poem. The opening verses (vv. 1-4) speak in almost identical terms of the vain search for truly righteous men in a corrupted community, a theme to be found in Jer. 5 : 1-5 in an ironic castigation of the failure of Jerusalem and its leaders. This is followed in 14 (vv. 5-6) with an interweaving of the themes of terror in judgement to the wicked and refuge and confidence for the righteous, while 53 (v. 5) lays all its stress on the theme of judgement and rejection of those opposed to his will. The difference is not great, yet one may get a glimpse even so of a different level of understanding. Then, in the final verse (14 : 7 = 52 : 6), the whole theme is lifted into a much wider plea to God to bring deliverance to his people by coming out from his holy place in Zion, restoring the fortunes of his people. This is a theme which frequently suggests the bringing back to their holy land of the scattered members of the community in time of exile and in the subsequent years, through the later biblical period and beyond, when many in other lands, in what is termed the Diaspora, the Dispersion, belonged to the community but were separated from it. The needs of the community and the anxieties at the lack of knowledge of God are thus taken up into a glorious hope of full restoration for the people of God. There is here a rich area of thought and source of confidence.

3

Poetry and Faith

THERE IS A saying attributed to Robert Browning. When asked the meaning of a passage in one of his poems, he replied: 'When I wrote that, God and Robert Browning knew what it meant; now only God knows'. Whether the story is true or not does not matter. It is, of course, told to suggest in a humorous manner that poetry is unintelligible, or at least that its precise meaning is not apparent. Yet one might wonder whether underlying the remark is the impatience of a poet at being asked to say what his poetry means, an impatience which stems from the realisation that readers so often suppose that poetry is only a difficult or odd way of writing prose. Put the words in a different order from usual, add the occasional rhyme, conform to a certain rhythmic pattern (or not even that if it is free verse you are writing), and there is a piece of poetry. But if a poet could say what he wanted to say in prose, he might just as well write that way. To those of us who are not poets, there is a mystery here which we can only begin to apprehend; the creative urge which forces ideas into a poetic shape is the prerogative of the poet. For us, the readers, the entry into that experience is through the poetic forms. Only thus can we penetrate the poet's realm of thought, his particular sense of reality, his apprehension of the meaning of what is thought or lived, his setting out of the impact of simple and everyday things or of the ultimate realities of love and sorrow, of death and of separation, of all that makes men most truly human and most conscious of both the dignity and

38

the fragility of life. All this the poet is endeavouring to say in the particular medium which he has chosen or which he knows to be imposed upon him.

Now we have already observed that with the psalms we are deprived of an obvious source of information about the meaning of what the poet has written. But perhaps it is not all loss. If we were in a position to ask the poet just what is meant by the words:

I have become like a bottle in the smoke (119 : 83)

he might reply as impatiently of our failure to understand as Robert Browning. We can try to unravel the simile. We can clarify it somewhat by suggesting that the reference is likely to be to a skin water bottle which would shrivel up when exposed to the smoke of a fire. We can then suppose that the whole line may be rendered: 'Even if I have become shrivelled up like a bottle in smoke, I do not forget your commandments', and observe that the context suggests other pictures for the distresses of the psalmist. But, when we have done this, there comes a point at which we need simply to go back to the words of the poem, render them as nearly as we may with faithfulness to their poetic language, and absorb the meaning suggested by the words. We cannot, indeed, here be sure that a particular line of interpretation is correct. Another rendering: 'I have wept like a wine-skin in the smoke' (Levi), perhaps pictures condensation on the outside of the cooled skin, suggesting weeping, a continuation of a theme found in the previous verse; and yet another supposes that the word rendered 'wine-skin' or 'bottle' really itself means 'to weep' or 'to grieve', though such a sense is very uncertain.

In this one example, we may see the double difficulty of language and custom that are remote and of poetic language which may, even when we understand the words and the thought-world, be allusive rather than precisely definable. Even when the imagery is sufficiently familiar for something of the thought to be conveyed, we need to be aware that a fuller exploration of the words and of the background to the ideas may lead to a greater clarification or to the correction of a misleading picture. A familiar psalm, which by the very simplicity of its language makes a direct appeal, may yield a richer content of thought when its imagery is explored. 23, best known of all the psalms, speaks clearly with its shepherd imagery, its themes of protection in places of danger, its confidence in lasting relationship with God. A closer examination may serve to draw out more, though inevitably such suggestions are tentative, depending on the degree to which subtlety is attributed to the poet's thought.

(Verse 1). The shepherd image—'God is my shepherd'—is simple enough, even though the loss of closeness to the countryside and its ways in much modern urban life dulls the edge of the analogy. We should also recall that the shepherd image is a standard one for the description of ancient rulers, and that tradition depicts the greatest king of Israel, David, in the guise of a shepherd boy chosen to be ruler. Are we perhaps being invited to see further the theme: God is shepherd to the king, the king is shepherd to his people? The prophet Micaiah saw 'all Israel scattered upon the mountains like a flock which has no shepherd' (1 Kings 22 : 17), a vivid symbol of judgement and disaster.

(Verse 2). The image is extended to feeding and pasturage. 'He makes me lie down in lush fields' and 'Beside the water in secure resting-places he guides me'. The common rendering 'still waters' creates an image of grassy fields and hardly moving water in a neighbouring stream; but the image is in reality linked to the theme of the giving of rest, of security. It is one which appears in relation to the people of God brought into the 'rest' of the promised land (95 : 11), an image also linked with the giving of rest, peace, from enemies (so Deut. 12 : 1; 2 Sam. 7 : 1). The stress lies upon plenty and safety, a suggestion thereby of the acknowledgement that what is needed for life and the security from danger which is necessary to community life are the gift of God. It is worth recalling that the king in Israel was seen as the one through whom the blessings of plenty and protection from enemies were mediated (cf. 72, especially vv. 8-11 and 16). (Verse 3a). 'He revives my life' or 'my person', a phrase which should probably be seen as linked with what precedes; the picture is of the shepherd bringing his flock to a good pasturage, with water in a secure place, and thereby reviving them, restoring them to full vigour.

(Verse 3b and c). Although the image of being led or guided provides a clear link with what precedes, we are in fact moving away from the shepherd image into a different area of thought. 'He leads me in right paths': we may begin from such a rendering, suggestive of the skill of the shepherd in ensuring the safety of his flock by the wisdom with which he manages them. But the word rendered 'right', used of what is fitting and proper, also suggests rightness of conduct, propriety of behaviour. So the phrase may suggest that way of life which is acceptable to God, and in which the poet knows himself to be led by God himself; it may also imply the way of victory or success. 'For the sake of his name' offers an explanation. The name of God is expressive of his nature; it is that by which he is invoked by his worshippers, but it is also indicative of what he is. Because God is God, the psalmist claims, prosperity, victory, is assured. The theme of security is lifted now into the wider political realm; the well-being of the community is suggested.

(Verse 4). 'Even if I must go through the darkest valley, I shall fear no disaster, because you are with me; it is your sceptre, your ruler's staff, which give me comfort'. The political realm of thought is present here, and in this verse and the next, two different aspects of God's protective power are brought out. Here the royal power of God is shown in what as ruler he bears: his sceptre, the mark of the king as he rules, and his ruler's staff, a term suggestive of security and support. To give comfort is to give strength, and this experience is contrasted with that of being in the realm of danger, of defeat. The phrase traditionally rendered 'valley of the shadow of death' may more simply mean 'valley of

41

great darkness', but carries with it the suggestion of the realm of death, of shadow and gloom, the realm of the powers felt to be ranged against God. Even in that realm the psalmist expresses his confidence in God's protection. Another psalmist expresses this in a vivid phrase: 'If I go up to the heavens, there you are; if I spread out my bed in Sheol (the realm of death), you are there too' (139 : 8); there is no escape from God's care. In 23, the theme of protection continues with the picture of a feast prepared in the presence of enemies (v. 5); the guest for whom God prepares the table is honoured, his head anointed with oil, his cup filled to overflowing. It is a triumphal scene. (Verse 6). God's blessing and loyalty to his worshipper, perhaps particularly to the king, is to be for ever; for the whole of a long life, which is what all men desire, he will be secure in the presence of God, in the temple where God makes himself known.

Robert Frost has said that 'poetry is that which is lost in translation'. There is truth in this, since to translate poetry from one language to another produces something new, however much it may be recognized as geared to the original. It is also an overstatement, since the enjoyment of translated poetry, whether of Homer or of the Bible or of Shakespeare, has been long known. But a more relevant meaning for Robert Frost's remark may be seen in what has just been offered by way of comment on 23. The explanation and paraphrase in the preceding paragraphs may well have produced the feeling that the poetry has been lost. Prosaic statements about shepherding and the realm of the dead and God's protective power, are no substitute for the poetry itself. If that were all the poet had been saying, then we might just as well put it in prose form. 'God is like a shepherd who tends his flock; the protection and care which he gives are to be experienced in triumph and well-being in every danger that threatens.' But it is not that which has made the psalm the best-known and for many the best-loved of all the psalms. It is the quality of the language, the pattern of phrases, the allusiveness of the statements. Explanation may take us back to the psalm able to detect the range of imagery more fully; it is no substitute for allowing the poetry to speak from poet to reader.

With this for the·psalms there goes something further. We cannot discover the original poet, we can only tentatively explore the possible original setting and meaning. For us, the psalms come in a context of interpretation, linked to the on-going life of the ancient Israelite people, renewed in the appreciation of the poetry in the context of Christian thought, enriched by the use of centuries, the imagery touched by the occasions to which it has been reapplied. For us, the modern readers, there must be a judicious combining of old and new. We must be true to the best understanding we may have of what the Hebrew poetry says and means, and let that speak to us of God. We may also share in the worship and reading of the centuries of use, knowing that we cannot detach our own reading of the psalms from that of our predecessors.

These more general comments on poetry and interpretation need some greater precision, and this is to be sought at various levels in the study of the structure of Hebrew poetry. This is an area which has many uncertainties, but a number of elements in the poetic structure may be seen clearly enough and appear sufficiently in translation to be appreciated.

1. *The smallest units of poetry.* It has long been recognized that particular effects are produced in Hebrew poetry, as in some other ancient poetry in related languages, by the arrangement of lines in parallel. Two short units often stand together, the sense of the one balanced by the sense of the other. Sometimes this is exact:

> hears/God/my entreaty
> God/my prayer/receives (6: 9)

The separate units of the Hebrew, three in each line, are marked off by the strokes; the Hebrew order is followed to show the precise structure. This parallelism is a fundamental element in Hebrew poetry. Its effect may be defined in terms of emphasis—the repeated idea is underlined; or of echo—the second line providing an answering statement to the first; or of development—the different words used in the second line in correspondence with those in the first providing a fuller picture of the poet's thought.

But such simple balance is only one such form. There is an immense range of correspondence. Another simple one is that of contrast:

> God indeed cares for/the way/of the righteous,
> but the way/of the wicked/is perishing. (1 : 6)

The use of the same word 'way' in both lines binds them together; the contrasts of righteous and wicked, and of care and perishing are stark. They underline the whole theme of the psalm to which this verse forms the climax. Or the second line may offer a development of the first:

> To God/belongs victory,
> upon your people/may your blessing be. (3 : 8)

The relationship of thought here is to be seen not in any precise parallel, though the words 'victory' and 'blessing' provide a good balance, and so too do 'God' and 'your people'. The link lies in the recognition that it is the God who is supreme in victory who is able to give blessing to his people; and indeed an alternative rendering of the verse would bring this out:

> O God of salvation,
> may your blessing be upon your people.

These are only some of the patterns. The marked division in such lines makes them very appropriate for that kind of use of the psalms in which by responsive reading or antiphonal singing the balancing elements are given a distinctive emphasis. But such rigid dividing of the lines may lose the poetry when the patterns are more complex, and this is immediately apparent where there are not two but three lines with a parallel of thought:

> The voice of God/is over the waters,
> the God of glory/thunders,
> God himself/over mighty waters. (29 : 3)

Here the echoes are more complex. 'Voice of God' and 'thunders' are linked since thunder as the sound of the divine voice is a common theme (e.g. John 12 : 28f.). There are echoes from 'voice of God' to 'God of glory' (with a different term for God) and 'God' (the word standing alone) in the third line. 'The waters' in the first line is picked up and extended by 'mighty waters' in the third.

There are other features of the structure of individual lines, though less certainly as to their precise nature. Much work still goes on to explore the nature of Hebrew poetry and the metrical patterns to which it operates; sufficient has been said here to indicate its richness.

2. *Groupings of lines.* We are already with this last example moving on into a slightly larger structure, and the possibilities become almost infinite. Groups of lines may form intricate patterns:

> Blessings for the man/who does not walk/in the counsel/of wicked men,
> nor in the way/of sinners/does he stand,
> nor in the seat of/the scornful/does he sit (1 : 1)

The first phrase stands alone; it will find its echo at the opening of the second part of the psalm: 'Not so the wicked' (v. 4). The three lines are neatly balanced: walk, stand, sit, all ways of expressing 'living'; counsel, way, seat; wicked, sinners, scornful, all provide correspondence.

45

Then/alive/they would have swallowed us,
in the burning/of their anger/against us,
then/the waters/would have swept us away,
the torrent/would have come over/ourselves,
then/would have come over/ourselves,
the waters/the seething ones. (124 : 3-5)

The repeated 'then' joins the units together. The enemies of
the psalmist swallow him up (see v. 2), an idea associated also
with Sheol, the realm of the dead, thought of as a monster
with open mouth—a picture often used in mediaeval wall-
paintings of the last judgement. This is echoed in the theme
of great and hostile waters, common symbol of the forces
ranged against God and his chosen ones. The third line with
its reference to waters is picked up in the sixth line with a
fuller description of the waters; and the intervening fourth
and fifth lines have closely similar wording. These last four
lines in fact provide an example of a common pattern,
known as chiasmus: the first and the last belong together in
sense, and so do the middle pair. It is yet another example
of the way in which a particular theme may be developed, by
repetition, by the echoing of words and ideas, by the gradual
building up of effect.

3. *Structure of a psalm.* The extension of such poetic
analysis to a whole psalm reveals the subtlety of the combining of words and ideas. 121 shows some interesting features:

I lift my eyes to the mountains.
  Whence comes *my help?*
  My help is from God,
maker of heaven and earth. (1-2)

He will not let your foot slip,
  nor will your guardian *sleep.*
  No he will not *sleep,* will not slumber,
the guardian of Israel. (3-4)

God is your guardian, God your shade,
   upon your right side.
   In *daytime* the sun will not smite you,
nor the moon at *night*. (5-6)

God will *guard* you from every ill,
   will *guard* your life.
   God will *guard* your daily life,
from now for ever. (7-8)

The translation attempts to draw out some of the subtlety. In
120-134, each psalm is given a title which means literally 'a
psalm for goings up', usually rendered 'ascents', possibly
psalms for pilgrimage. A number of these psalms have what
we may describe as a stair-like pattern. A word in one line is
echoed by a word in the next; and the underlining here is to
draw attention to this. It is not always clear in translation because it is not necessarily elegant to translate the same word
or a related word by the same word in English. Thus
'guardian' and 'guard' correspond to related words in Hebrew,
but 'watchman' would more nearly give the picture, since the
word is used of the watchman of a city; and the verb may
have the meaning 'preserve', 'protect'. This echo effect may
be lost in translation, but its effect is to bind the psalm
closely together, giving it an overall unity which derives from
the gradual unfolding of a series of themes concerning God's
protection of his people.

8 shows other aspects of such structuring. It begins and
ends with the same line:

O God our lord, how majestic your name throughout the
   earth. (vv. 1a, 9)

Mention of 'the heavens' in 1b is echoed at the end of the
psalm in v. 8 'the birds of the heavens', and also in v. 3. That
the heavens are the 'works of God's fingers' in v. 3 is picked
up in the corresponding phrase in v. 6 'you make him ruler
over the works of your hands'. The majesty of God in vv. 1

and 9 contrasts with the status of man in v. 4; and that status of man contrasts with the exalted position given to man by God as ruler over all that God has made in vv. 5-8.

Psalms with refrains, such as 42-43, or 46, or 107, provide fuller examples of such interlinking of thought. Not infrequently, as in 107, the refrain does not appear each time with identical wording; the effect is more that of an echo than of repetition. Nor is the refrain merely a marker at the end of a section of the poem; it serves to draw together the thought, and relates to the context in which it stands. In 46, where the refrain appears in vv. 7 and 11, it should almost certainly stand also after v. 3. Then each section of the psalm underlines a different aspect of divine power and protection. The insecurity of the whole world-order in vv. 1-3 is set in contrast with the exalted stronghold which is God. Palestine is in an earthquake area so that the reality of such insecurity is familiar to the poet (cf. Amos 1 : 1; Zech. 14 : 5). The life-giving power of God in his holy city (cf. Ezek. 47) stands over against the tumult of the nations (cf. 2 : 1-6); and thereby the exalted stronghold which is God is seen in relation to that holy city which he has chosen. The warfare of God against alien forces and his exaltation over all nations and over all the world brings us to a climax in the recognition that this is our God, our exalted stronghold.

4. *Forms of psalmody.* For centuries it has been recognized that there are different kinds of psalms—thanksgivings, acts of praise, acts of confession and penitence, expressions of trust and confidence. Some appear to be spoken by individual worshippers, some by the whole community or by a spokesman on its behalf. In recent years much attention has been devoted to defining these and other particular forms more closely. By examining each example of a particular kind of psalm, it is possible to trace the elements of which such a psalm will be composed. Thus a type which is usually for convenience called a 'hymn' consists of three elements: an initial summons to praise:

Come let us acclaim God,
    let us make a shout to the rock of our salvation.
    (95 : 1)

The second section provides the motivation for such praise, often introduced with an explanatory 'for':

For supreme God is our God,
    even supreme king over all gods. (95 : 3)

a statement followed in vv. 4-5 with statements of his creative activity and his control of the world. This in its turn is followed by a statement of praise or blessing or prayer (95 : 6).

Analysis of this kind has both its strengths and its weaknesses. It shows clearly how close the structure of many of the psalms is to their counterparts—hymns or laments or thanksgivings—in the ancient near east. It helps us to understand the movement of the psalmist's thought and the degree to which he is controlled in his poetic composition by standard patterns. It also helps us to appreciate the many stereotyped phrases which are used, the similarity of style and content which marks so many psalms. On the other hand, the impression must not be given that the psalms are all much of a muchness. There is richness and variety in the handling of these patterns, and what has already been said about the combining of elements into a liturgical structure is important for our understanding of many of them. 95, just quoted, in fact moves on from the hymnic opening into warning and exhortation in vv. 7-11, the psalmist drawing lessons from the traditions of his people to exhort a true response in worship.

In addition, many of the problems of psalm interpretation are not answered by the study of poetic structure. Psalms which speak of national distress—like 44—clearly respond to the needs of the whole community. But we do not know who spoke such words on the people's behalf. Was it the king during the period of the monarchy; or perhaps a cultic

49

D

official who could be understood to speak for the king? When a psalm appears to express the distress of an individual or to speak in the first person singular in praise or thanksgiving, we cannot be sure whether this is really a prayer spoken by a single worshipper, or whether here too we may have the wider needs of the community expressed in this highly personal manner. Furthermore, as we have seen, the process of reinterpretation brought changes, so that psalms belonging to one situation were seen to be meaningful in another. This is where we must again move away from the mere attempt at discovering origins—whether in actual concrete situations or in the particular moments of ancient worship—and look at the function which such psalms come in course of tim to perform. And again we may see that such a tran formation of psalmody over the centuries, essential to its continuing use, sets our contemporary reading and use in the context of a long tradition of seeing in these poems insights into the nature and purpose of God and the realities of human experience.

While all parts of the biblical text have been subject to interpretation and reinterpretation, this is particularly evident for the poetry. The allusiveness of poetic language, the metaphors, the interweaving of ideas, all encourage the discovery of new meanings. There is an interplay here between psalmist and reader and tradition. The appropriation of the psalmist's poetic statement calls for an appreciation of where that poetry stands in relation to the great themes of Israel's theology, and how over a long period of time they were re-applied to the needs of individual and community within the Old Testament: and how beyond that they have enabled later readers, bo Jews and Christians, to gain deeper insight both into the religious tradition in which they stand and into the particular moments of their own experience and their own contemporary situation.

4

Theology through the Psalms

ANY ATTEMPT AT writing an ordered and systematic account of the theology of the Bible or, more particularly, of the Old Testament, comes up against the difficulty that the material does not easily lend itself to neat arrangement. If we try, we are liable to impose on a rich and varied literature a pattern which belongs to our own ways of thinking. What is true of the whole is true also of the parts. The Psalter provides so very wide a range of insights into what may be said about God and about the relationships between man and God, that there is artificiality in treating this particular collection of poems as if it were a rounded whole. It is a variegated collection and we may miss the variety if we set out a too orderly picture of its thought.

Here is an advantage of those systems of using the psalms which take them simply in order, since this may let them speak for themselves. It does not follow from this that there is any particular merit in reading several psalms in a row merely because it is found convenient to have a regular number of verses. Long psalms get broken up; short psalms get read as an unco-ordinated bunch, and the lack of observable connection between a psalm and the one that precedes and follows makes it difficult to see why we should read them together. As we have already seen, this difficulty is already present also in the fact that some psalms clearly consist of more than one element; and again that some psalms have traditionally or in certain circles been divided into more than one separate section. We cannot therefore expect that any particular psalm will necessarily contain only one theme, and this is a weakness in any attempt at finding a single phrase which will serve as a title for a psalm or as a guide to its meaning, though such a phrase may sometimes help us to distinguish one of its lines of thought. Nor should we suppose that at any one reading we shall be able to discover the whole range of thought that is opened up. The disclosure of what the poetry is saying will come only as we read and re-read.

The present chapter attempts no more than an opening up of some themes and of some psalms. For fuller insights the psalms must themselves be read; and with the help of commentaries and other studies more and more of insight may come. A relationship needs to be established between the psalms, speaking with a quality which is not limited to a particular moment in time or to a particular situation and, ourselves as readers, in the particular moment and in the particular situation in which we find ourselves on a specific occasion of reading.

The method adopted here is simply that of suggesting some of the lines of thought which may emerge from the chosen psalms and in this, to consider some of the major areas of religious thought which appear again and again in the psalms. The reading of a single psalm or of a passage from a psalm may bring us afresh into one of these larger areas with perhaps some new insight into its meaning for us.

Psalm 19 begins with general statements about the revelation of God and his works in the heavens which enclose the world of man.

> The heavens are telling the glory of God,
>   that which his hands have made, the firm vault
>   of the sky relates.
> Day to day pours out the message,
>   night to night makes the knowledge plain. (19 : 1-2)

The contemplation of the sky here, as the second part of the psalm shows (vv. 7-11), evokes the recognition of man's status in relation to God. Another psalm makes the point more fully:

> When I look at your heavens, the works of your fingers,
>> moon and stars which you have set securely in place,
> then what is man that you should keep him in mind,
>> a mere human being that you should take account of
>>> him? (8 : 3-4)

The opening of 19 uses participles to express the continuing nature of the witness of the skies to God's glory; it is a device commonly to be found in hymnic passages which speak of creation. What God does belongs not to past, present or future but to the eternity which transcends time. Thus 136 invokes the praise of God:

> to the one alone doing great wonders,
>> to the one making the heavens in wisdom,
>>> to the one beating out the surface of the
>>>> earth upon the waters. (136 : 4-6)

It offers an easy move over from statement of God's creative action—'So God made the vault of the sky and divided the waters which were below that vault from those that were above it' (Gen. 1 : 7)—to the description of God as creator, 'maker of heaven and earth'. The distinction is an important one, for it moves away from the mechanical concept of God as having supposedly created the world at a moment in the past; it proposes an understanding of the relationship between God and the world which is continually in being.

The thought of these opening verses of 19 is interwoven. What day and night reveal—'the message' (literally 'word'), and 'the knowledge'—exemplifies the phrases 'glory of God' and 'that which his hands have made'. The glory of God is that expression of his being which may be known to men in the terror of judgement, in the awareness of a power which reaches far beyond the human sphere (cf. Isa. 6). When it is expressed in terms of 'knowledge', there is brought out the reality of a relationship which may be more fully described as 'knowledge of God', intimacy of relationship with him; as 'fear of God', the propriety of a due sense of awe at who he is. These are expressions which we might translate as 'religion', that appreciation of the relationship which seeks to express it in terms of belief and of worship. The Old Testament uses the same verb of 'knowing' God, in this rich sense of awareness and contact, as also of the relationship between man and woman in sexual encounter. If the full explanation of this latter usage remains not entirely clear, there is evident here a sense of the analogy between the mysteries of human relationships at their deepest levels and those of man's encounter with God in his religion.

> Without speech, without words,
>   without their voice being heard,
>   through all the earth their cry goes out,
>   to the very end of the world their words. (19 : 3-4b)

To some commentators verse 3 has appeared as a prosaic comment, designed to correct a literal understanding of the opening lines. When poetry is read as if it were prose, a reader may be tempted to ask in what language the heavens are supposed to speak. But an awareness of the poetic quality of the opening lines makes such a question irrelevant. The poet in fact picks up from verse 2 the word there rendered 'message' and here translated 'speech' and affirms the universal presence of a message which can be apprehended without it being articulated in the forms of human speech. There is a neat contrast between the firm denial of literal speech ('without speech, without words') and the final phrase underlining the reality of the message (using another Hebrew term for 'words' from that used in the opening).

The general setting thus pictured paves the way for a more precise statement:

For the sun a tent is set up in them (the heavens),
    he is like a bridegroom who comes out from his
        wedding canopy,
    he rejoices like a warrior to run his course.
From one end of the heavens is his rising,
    his circuit reaches to their furthest ends,
    nothing is hidden from his heat. (19 : 4c-6)

It has sometimes been supposed that the first half of this
psalm is really an ancient poem directed to a sun god, taken
over by Israel and re-interpreted by the addition of the
second part dealing with the law. Probably we should recognize the use in these lines of metaphors linked ultimately with
beliefs about the divine nature and power of the sun. Such
beliefs are very understandable as arising from the recognition of the relationship between the sun and the daytime,
when release from the fears of darkness is given; and between
the sun and life and death, which recognizes both the life-
giving power of warmth and the death-dealing force of intense
heat. The story of the woman of Shunem's child in 2 Kings 4
(cf. vv. 18f.) provides an example of the latter, a theme also
alluded to in Ps. 91 : 6 and 121 : 6. Imagery connected with a
mythology of the sun appears here in the use of the bridegroom and warrior imagery. We know that Israel was familiar
with such ideas from references to the removal of symbols
of sun-worship from the temple at Jerusalem (2 Kings 23 : 11)
and in all probability also from some of the elements in the
Samson stories which are comparable with material found in
mythology elsewhere. But here in this psalm, the sun has
become an image for the all-seeing God. The heavens provide
the setting for the sun, whose vitality and life-giving qualities
may be compared with those of the bridegroom, and whose
daily running of his course through the sky is like the strength
of the warrior (cf. Ahimaaz in 2 Sam. 18 : 19-23). Their
proclamation of the glory of God (vv. 1-4b) links them to the
revealing of that God whose all-seeing power is untiring and
ever-renewed.

It is in this context that the psalmist turns to the theme of man's life. In effect, though without spelling the matter out, he has been proclaiming in the opening verses not simply the glory of God, but the order of the world which is God's creation. That order itself testifies to God. So the analogy is presented by which we may understand the requirements laid down for man, the law of God which is God's directive to man, his covenant obligation laid upon Israel, the way of life by which the obedient may find themselves in close contact with God. The verses which follow (7-11) unfold the nature and meaning of that law. Several features of this exposition may be drawn out. In vv. 7-9 six different words are used for the law; they serve both to elaborate the meaning and to suggest completeness. A much more elaborate form is to be found in 119 where virtually every line of the psalm contains a synonym for the law. Man's life, it is being affirmed, lies in the fullness of that revelation of God's directives for him and of God's provision for every aspect of what he is and does. Among these terms there are more general ones: 'law' and 'testimony' (v. 7), terms often used to denote the whole requirement of what God lays down, the latter also associated with the king (2 Kings 11 : 12), apparently as expressive of specific responsibilities before God. There are others that are more precise: 'statutes' or requirements and 'commandment' (v. 8), the latter more often used in the plural to refer to particular obligations; 'legal decisions' (v. 9), which suggest particularly the confidence that what God decrees maintains what is just and especially the rights of the unprotected such as widows and orphans. The expression 'fear of God' (v. 9) suggests, like 'knowledge of God', the whole right relationship with God which belongs to his faithful.

Then we may note how the emphasis lies here on that fullness of life which stems from the acceptance of what God decrees. This draws out a contrast with what is often supposed to be the idea of law in the Old Testament. Criticism of a legal approach to religion—a belief that by right actions, conformity to a certain standard, a man can get credit with God—runs through the Old Testament as clearly as it does the New, and finds its place equally in Jewish thinking. That is not what law is about in the Old Testament, and the psalm makes it clear. Law is the term, often better explained as directive or requirement, which sets out the way of life which is in conformity with God's purposes and which can therefore be described sharply in terms of 'way of life' rather than its opposite 'way of death' (cf. Deut. 30 : 15-20). That many of the requirements of the Old Testament law are expressed in ways which belong to a particular context and a particular social and religious system does not alter that fundamental point. The Old Testament shows itself fully aware of the fact that men's understanding of what God requires changes with a deepening apprehension of who he is; and it shows itself also sensitive to the deeper problem of how men can know, if indeed they can, exactly what it is that God requires, what is this way of life. The New Testament reveals the same awareness of change and the same sensitivity to the problem of knowledge. But in neither case is there any doubt that the true life of man belongs here, in obedience to the will of God.

The psalm section closes with the reminder of this.

> Even your servant is warned by them,
>   in observance of them is great reward. (19 : 11)

The law of God sets limits to a man's behaviour and defends him from disaster; it offers reward—the term used suggests that which follows on, a sequel to a right relationship. Often, throughout the Bible, such reward is described in material terms. It is understandable that this should be so since it is difficult to bring out the nature of reward in other ways. The inequalities of human life call out much questioning about this, and the psalms are often concerned with the matter, particularly where they contrast the prosperity of the wicked with the needs of the righteous. Complaint at what appears to be injustice issues sometimes in violence of language against the wicked (so for example 109), but also in reflection

57

on life and its meaning in such psalms as 49 and 73. In part at least, Old Testament thought here shows its concentration on the realities of life, and life in this world. But the problem of reward and punishment is not resolved by supposing that the balance can be redressed in another life. That undermines the proper recognition of the world and its life as the sphere of God's creation and re-introduces the idea of obedience to gain credit with God by shifting the moment at which credit will be recognized into a life beyond death. Here in 19 : 11 the conviction is proclaimed that life here and now may be within the way of the law, and obedience itself offers the way of life. There is no other motive.

The contemplation of order in the world and of the possibility opened up by God's law of order in the life of man leads the psalmist into his final concerns.

> Unwitting sins, who can know?
>   Keep me innocent of hidden ones.
> Even from acts of defiance restrain your servant.
>   Do not let them control me.
> So let me be blameless,
>   innocent of any great sin. (19 : 12-13)

The problem of obedience is seen to be both in knowing oneself and in knowing what is required. The problem lies both in unrecognized failure and in the defiant flouting of God's will which belongs to human experience. And the negative anxieties of these verses find their counterpart in positive appeal:

> Let the words of my mouth be acceptable,
>   the thinking of my mind be in your presence,
>   O God, my rock and my redeemer. (19 : 14)

Acceptability to God and the possibility of being in the presence of God belong together. 15 is one of a number of psalms and psalm passages which express concern at what may exclude a man from the presence of God, cut off the right of entry to the shrine where God chooses to make himself known. In asking that he may be acceptable to God, his life in conformity with the law which he has described in such loving terms, he takes us back to the beginning of the psalm. The glory of God which the heavens reveal is the very being of that God who is often described as the 'rock' (e.g. Deut. 32 : 4; 1 Sam. 2 : 2)—symbol of protection, of shelter, of firmness—and as 'redeemer', the term used with reference to the deliverance of Israel from bondage in Egypt but also more broadly of the kinsman who has responsibility for the protection of those who belong within the same family. Jeremiah, redeeming the piece of family land which is in danger of alienation, as surely defends the position of the family to which he belongs (Jer. 32), as God, as redeemer, confirms the security in his power of the people that he has called to be his own.

19 shows how little we may set out a systematic treatment of the religious thought of the psalms. It attests the recognition of God as creator, with particular emphasis on the relationship between his creator status and the knowledge of his nature and his all-controlling providence. It points to the ordering of the life of the world and its counterpart in the ordering of the life of Israel under God's law. Without any direct allusion to the great moments of Israel's history, it thus affirms the relevance of the giving of the law, and reflects upon its quality in the lives of men. It shows a concern with the problems of knowledge of God and of his will for men, while portraying richness of life under the law. It appeals for help in the business of living, making appeal to the God who is both protector and kinsman to his people.

[Other psalms in which these and related themes are explored are: 1, 8, 24, 33, 65, 90, 104, 145.]

Psalm 47 begins with a summons to all the people of the world:

> All nations, clap your hands,
>   acclaim God with the sound of a shout. (47 : 1)

Worship is often thought of merely in terms of suitably moderated voices and orderly behaviour. There is a proper place for this, since worship must be a reality expressive of the people that offer it and not an artificially contrived performance. But for Israel such constraint would have seemed too limiting. The clapping of hands as an act of welcome to the deity; the blowing of the ram's horn to announce a celebration; the raising of a shout of welcome to the God who makes his presence known—all these and more are seen as the normal accompaniments of psalmody. The acclamation of God is the same whether he comes to his people in the moment of religious celebration in the shrine, or in the hour of battle, symbolised by the presence of his Ark (1 Sam. 4 : 5). Here the summons is for his acknowledgement as God by all peoples. The reason for the acclaim follows:

> For
> God is the exalted one, the terrible,
> supreme king over all the earth. (47 : 2)

The title 'exalted one' or 'Most High' is often associated with Jerusalem, and may be a title which came to be applied to Israel's God at the time that Jerusalem became the shrine of the united kingdom under David and Solomon. It serves here to point to the absolute supremacy of God. Often this is expressed in terms of the supremacy of God over all other gods (e.g. 95 : 3 where we find exactly comparable wording: 'supreme king over all gods'). Indeed, such a thought is the counterpart to what is said here, for the gods of all nations can be understood to be acknowledging the supreme God as their ruler.

The relationship of the nations to God is developed in the theme of Israel's own status:

> He subdued nations beneath us,
> and peoples under our feet.
> He chose for us our heritage,
> the pride of Jacob whom he loves. (47 : 3-4)

The theme of Israel's history provides a basis for present confidence and hope. Sometimes with quite explicit statement (so for example in such a great historical survey as 78), more often with brief allusion, as here, we are reminded of one of the central elements of Israel's faith. The people traces its origin and its full life as the people of God to the faith that God at a moment of time in the past declared his intentions to Israel by an act of deliverance from slavery in Egypt, by the establishing in the desert of a covenant with them, and by the gift of the promised land of Canaan. The themes are most fully elaborated in the wealth of story and law now to be found in the books Exodus to Numbers, and again in Deuteronomy and Joshua. They form an important element in prophetic thought, as the basis for an appeal to Israel to respond to God's demands. They provide the main basis for historical allusion in the psalms, where there is little reference to the stories of the earlier heroes—Abraham, Isaac and Jacob (cf. 105 for an exception)—and little direct allusion to the stories of the judges or kings, even David (83 and 132 provide examples of these). For the psalmists, the great moment is that of exodus, wilderness and conquest; it provides a pattern for thinking about the experiences of a later age (especially clearly too in Isa. 40-55), as indeed it provides a pattern also for New Testament thought about the action of God in Christ. So here in 47 we are reminded of the subduing of the nations of Canaan in verse 3, and of the choice of Israel's heritage, a common term for the land which is seen as representing Israel's family inheritance, a land designed to belong to the people and to be closely associated with their status as a people. The word 'pride' used in parallel with this description of the land suggests the same point: it is this possession of the land which provides an assured basis for the people's life. In ancient Hebrew thought a man, and hence equally a people, without land is 'an empty person' (so of the landless followers of Jephthah in Judges 11 : 3).

Thus, as frequently in the Old Testament, praise for God by the nations of the world is called for both because of the awesome sovereignty of God (v. 2) and for his acts of care in the establishment of Israel as his people (vv. 3-4). It is when the nations see what God has done that they will respond to what he is, and this may be expressed either in terms of God's deliverance of his people from Egypt and his bringing of them into Canaan—so the confession of faith put into the mouth of Rahab at Jericho (Josh. 2 : 9-11)—or in terms of his bringing back his people from exile, his re-establishment of them as his people—so in the declaration of God's glory among the nations when Israel's punishment for failure and their restoration because of God's love are observed (Ezek. 39 : 21-29).

The act of praise at God's supremacy continues:

> God has gone up with a shout,
>   our God at the sound of the horn.
> Sing praises, O gods, sing praises,
>   sing praises to our king, sing praises.
> For king of all the earth is God;
>   sing a psalm in his honour. (47 : 5-7)

The picture is of God as king ascending his throne, honoured by his subjects who are his worshippers. The sound of the ram's horn marks the moment of celebration. God is acclaimed as king of the whole world; he has, as it were, taken over the rule of the nations, and we may see here the significance of the line which, as here translated, refers to the 'gods', that is the gods of the nations summoned to praise God. In 82 we find a vivid portrayal of God as supreme judge in the heavenly court condemning the gods to death 'as ordinary men' (so 82 : 7) for their failure to maintain justice, and so the call

> Arise, O God, judge the world,
>   for it is you who inherit all nations (82 : 8)

The rendering given here for 47 : 6 is not certain, but it makes excellent sense in the context. The nations are to acknowledge God; the deities that they worship and to whom they turn for protection and blessing, themselves become subjects of God as the supreme ruler of heaven and earth. Nor is the final phrase of verse 7 easy to understand, but it suggests the offering to God of a particular kind of psalm, and one which may perhaps best be associated with the establishment of the absolute kingship of God.

The theme continues in the final verses:

> God is king over all nations,
> God sits enthroned upon his holy throne.
> The rulers of the nations assemble,
> as the people of the God of Abraham.
> Indeed to God belong the rulers of the earth.
> Supremely exalted! (47 : 8-9)

The enthroned deity is acclaimed, greeted with a formula associated with the welcome accorded to a newly acknowledged king (so of Absalom in 2 Sam. 15 : 10). The rulers, with whom their peoples are associated, are described as actually becoming God's people, associated with the traditions of God's ancient calling of Abraham to be the founder of his people. They are, as it were, adopted into the one community. Small wonder that the psalm ends with an interjection of praise, acknowledging God to be the supremely exalted one.

Such a psalm as this—and there are a considerable number which make direct or implicit allusion to the kingship of God —makes use of ideas associated with the king in Israel. Theological statements are often couched in language expressive of the social or political organisation of the community which makes the statements. For our own understanding of their meaning, we need both to appreciate the particular social and political situation and to translate it into our own terms. For Israel, the king stood in a particular relationship to both God and people. The acknowledgement of the king by the people and their acceptance of his rule were an important element in this. The king was seen as the upholder of law and justice, and as a final court of appeal in difficult cases. So too God could be described as the accepted ruler, the ultimate giver of law and the upholder of justice.

The political situation had another dimension: during much of their history, the kingdoms of Israel and Judah came under the control of great imperial powers, the powers of Assyria and Babylonia in particular. The understanding of the ruler of such an empire as the great king, the supreme one, suggested, as we can see in 47, the picture of God as king of kings, supreme ruler of all nations. Israel and its king came under the protection of God as this supreme ruler. But this also produced a further extension of thought. The relationship between God and his chosen king—for so the individual kings as well as the whole dynasty of David came to be understood—pointed to the further understanding of that king's function. As the anointed one of God he could be seen as God's agent, God's ruler on earth. The court language of the ancient world, as of more modern times, could speak of the king in extravagant ways. 'O king, live for ever' is one such expression. The king as victor over all his enemies is another. The king as ruler on behalf of God could be understood to be ideally the ruler of all nations; subjecting themselves to God, they become subject to the king (so very clearly in 2 : 10-12). The term 'anointed one' was given a re-interpretation, to point not to an actually reigning king of David's line but to a coming ruler divinely chosen, a Messiah—which means 'an anointed one' and which, applied to Jesus, is translated into Greek as Christ. So the understanding of the king as ruler over all nations, as agent of God; the acknowledgement by the nations of God as supreme, and of his king as acting on his behalf, provided a basis for ways in which the action of God in Christ could be set out.

[Other psalms which may be read in this context include 2, 8, 29, 66, 67, 72, 89, 93, 97-99, 115.]

Psalm 80 presents the appeal of king and people for restoration to well-being in a time of distress. A broad appeal for help (vv. 1-7) is followed by a poetic description of the people's historic experience of God's action (vv. 8-11), and leads into a more specific call for help (vv. 12-19). The various parts of the psalm are closely bound together by a refrain which appears in vv. 3, 7 and 19, but which is echoed also in vv. 4 and 14.

> O shepherd of Israel, hear us,
>> you who lead Joseph like a flock.
> You who are enthroned on the cherubim shine out
>> to the people of Ephraim and Benjamin.
> From sleep stir up your might
>> and come to victorious action for us.
> O God restore us,
>> let your face shine toward us that we may be victorious. (80 : 1-3)

The shepherd theme, more fully developed in 23, is here used more deliberately of God as king and God as the leader of his people. The theme of protection is balanced by that of summons to warlike action against enemies. God as king is enthroned on the cherubim—winged lions as symbols of the deity's throne, a part of the furnishing of the inner shrine of the temple at Jerusalem (described in 1 Kings 6 : 23-28), and related to pictures of kings on their thrones in the ancient near east. Appeal is made to him to reveal himself, to shine out in his splendour, making his presence and his power known to his people. The references to Israel and Joseph in v. 1 and to Ephraim and Benjamin in v. 2 (where the Hebrew text in fact also has a reference to Manasseh), suggest that the psalm, or this part of it, was originally associated with the northern kingdom rather than with Jerusalem. So we have here a small clue to the way in which the later worship of the one central shrine at Jerusalem made use of psalms which originally belonged to another holy place. The translation

E

given here follows a commonly accepted small emendation by which the name 'Manasseh', which does not fit well into the poetic structure, is read to mean 'from sleep'—the same letters in Hebrew in a different order—and joined to the next phrase. The picture is a bold one; a vivid form of it is found in 78 : 65, where it is said that:

> God awoke like one who sleeps,
> like a warrior shouting when he is drunk.

The worshippers, in the urgency of their distress, feel that God has so withdrawn himself from them as if he were asleep. 121, we have seen (p. 46), stresses the unsleeping watchfulness of God. Elijah, mocking the prophets who call upon the alien god Baal, taunts them by suggesting that they should 'call louder . . . for perhaps he is asleep and must be wakened' (1 Kings 18 : 27). An image may be used in a variety of ways; its limitations as well as its effectiveness must be in our minds as we read. To one who suffers, the indifference of God or his angry withdrawal or his unapproachability may all seem evident. Like Job, he may at one and the same time cry out in violent language against God who treats him with malice and express in passionate terms his longing for the same God in whom alone is his life. Religion is not expressed only in neat and sober formulas of belief.

The power of God for victory is associated both with his showing himself in glory and in his expression of favour—his face shining towards his worshippers (cf. the priestly blessing of Num. 6 : 24-26). The first element of the refrain: 'O God restore us', expresses the desire for a change of fortune, a change from defeat to victory, from disaster to well-being, from poverty to prosperity. It is here separated from the title 'God of hosts' which appears as the opening of the next verse, but associated with the desire for favour and victory which is its third element.

O God of hosts
> how long will you be obdurate towards your
> people's prayer?

You have made them eat bread of tears,
> made them drink tears in full measure.

You have made us a derision to our neighbours,
> and our enemies mock us.

O God of hosts restore us,
> let your face shine towards us that we may be
> victorious. (80 : 4-7)

Again we see the boldness of poetic language. The anguish of distress appears in the phrase 'how long', a common element in psalms of lamentation (cf. e.g. 79 : 5); it expresses despair at what appears to be God's inactivity, or his anger, or his unwillingness to pay heed to his people's need. There is no measurement of time here; 'how long' may be said in the moment of distress regardless of actual duration. It may express the anguish of a single disaster equally with the prolonged desolation of years of exile or subjection to an alien power. Even more extreme is the suggestion of 'be obdurate', or perhaps 'resist', in the face of the urgent prayers offered to him for help. That God should refuse to hear is to be seen as the inversion of a positive assertion about him. If the deity were capricious, never to be relied on for any consistent response, then men would be at his mercy without hope of understanding. The distress for the psalmist lies in his deep-rooted conviction that the God who appears thus withdrawn from his people is the God who is their shepherd and their king. Distress and the agony of separation from God are expressed further in the metaphorical language of food and drink as tears, and in the probably equally metaphorical language of mockery.

The theme of enemies appears in v. 6. We may note a change in form. Up till now, the psalmist has spoken of 'your people', 'them'. Now he identifies himself as one of the people, one of 'us'. Such changes of person are frequent in

Hebrew poetry. Often, as here, they provide vividness and emphasis. It is not specified who the enemies are. They appear frequently in the psalms, mocking at the distresses of God's people or deriding those of the individual worshipper. Such a reference may be to political enemies, the surrounding nations or the great powers with which Israel was frequently involved in conflict. The references to military might and to victory in the opening verses of the psalm make this possible. But such language is a ready metaphor for any kind of distress, and what may have originated in one area of man's experience comes to be readily applicable to other experiences both outward—the failure of harvest, the illness of the individual—and inward—the moments of uncertainty such as the death of a king, the distresses of personal grief and fear of death. Fear, whether of the known or the unknown, and insecurity, remain areas of experience universally shared.

These verses open with the appeal to God as 'God of hosts' and end with the full refrain, also containing these words. The expression is a frequent one in the Old Testament. It suggests the heavenly assembly, the hosts of heaven as the attendant beings surrounding and supporting the supreme God. It thus becomes a title for God, and is often transliterated in liturgical poems and hymns as *Sabaoth*, for example in the confession of faith known as the *Te Deum*. It may also denote the heavenly bodies, sun, moon and stars, depicted as attendant on God, or as fighting on his behalf. So in Judges, 5 : 20:

> From heaven they fought,
>   the stars from their orbits,
>   fought against Sisera.

Hence it may be rendered 'God of armies', which points also to the third level of meaning in which God is depicted as the commander of the armies of his people, a theme particularly fully developed in the stories of Israel's conquest of Canaan (cf. especially Josh. 5 : 13-15 and in the psalms, especially

44). The relationship between God and his people is often expressed in such a way as to suggest that the enemies of God are also the enemies of Israel (cf. Judges 5 and especially v. 31 for a vivid presentation of this theme). It is an idea fully intelligible in a world in which the association between a deity and the community which worships him is often felt to be very close, so that the fortunes of both are thought to be bound together. When the kingdom of Judah fell to Babylonian power, there were those who saw this as defeat also for the God whom they worshipped. Deeper understanding led to the recognition that God and people cannot be so bound, and God's freedom to repudiate a covenant broken by the people's disobedience must make the relationship a less simple one. It led also to the realisation, as the Old Testament came to affirm ever more clearly the sole reality of one God, that political events must be viewed from within the wider purposes of God. A nation which identifies its policies with the will of God must in the end be forced to the recognition that its view of God is too small, its understanding of its policies too parochial.

The next part of the psalm may be seen to develop aspects of this deeper understanding.

> A vine from Egypt you pulled up,
>> you drove out nations and planted it.
> You made a clear space before it,
>> you made it root itself well,
>>> and so you made it fill the land.
> Mountains were covered with its shade,
>> its branches were as mighty cedars.
> It sent out its shoots to the sea
>> and its suckers to the river. (80 : 8-11)

The picture of Israel as a vine or a vineyard is a favourite one in the Old Testament (cf. e.g. Isa. 5 : 1-7; Ezek. 19 : 10-14), taken up and re-used in the New (cf. e.g. Mark 12 : 1-9; John 15 : 1-9). Like any poetic analogy, its detail must not be pressed, and we may observe how elements of the picture—the planting of the vine—are combined with elements from Israel's history—the driving out of the nations. The flourishing of the people in Canaan is suggested by the picture being stretched so that the vine becomes of enormous size, as great as the 'cedars of God', which may, as translated above, mean 'mighty cedars' and hence the great cedar trees of Lebanon, noted for their stature and spread (cf. Isa. 2 : 13); but it may imply something greater still, trees of a kind fit only for the world which God inhabits, such as might be found in the garden of God. The heightening of effect is carried further with the spreading out of branches above ground and shoots below ground to the sea—which can mean the Mediterranean —and the river—which is sometimes used quite simply for the Euphrates. A political interpretation of this may be seen in the attributing to David of rule over so wide an area as this (e.g. 2 Sam. 8 : 3). But it is more likely that we should here think of 'Sea' and 'River', using capital letters to suggest that these are names designating the great waters believed to lie at the edges of the earth. What we then have is a picture of the extension of Israel's domain, and hence God's domain, to the very ends of the earth. It is another way of making the point that through his choice of Israel and his love for this one people, God declares his purpose for all nations and his rule over the whole earth.

But now the mood changes:

> Why have you broken down its walls
> so that all who pass along the road can pluck it?
> The wild boars of the thickets gnaw at it,
> wild things of the countryside feed on it. (80 : 12-13)

The prophet Isaiah, using this same picture of the vineyard, had a very clear answer to the question: it is the failure of the people of God to produce true fruits of justice and righteousness, in spite of all the care which he had lavished upon them, that will lead to his breaking down the protecting walls and allowing the wild beasts free range (Isa. 5 : 1-7). No such explanation is given here. An experience of disaster, of whatever kind, has raised questions about the activity of God. The disaster has been interpreted as due to the direct action of God, but no explanation is offered for it in precise terms. What does appear is the underlying reliance of the people on God and his purposes. What he has been to his people, he still is, and hope lies in his unchanging purpose.

> O God of hosts, turn please,
>> look from heaven and see,
> pay heed to this vine,
>> restore what your right hand planted.
> May those who set fire to it, who destroyed it,
>> perish at the wrath which you show. (80 : 14-16)

The refrain appears here again in part, though modified in such a way as to call upon God to turn round. He is pictured as having turned his face away from his people, showing hostility to them: he is invited to turn round so that his face is towards them, a sign of favour. Israel, as the vine planted by God, is seen as his especial care, and appeal is made to him to have a regard for what he himself established. Favour to Israel is to be accompanied by judgement against those who brought disaster to God's people. There is again no specification of who is involved. What may have begun in precise reference to particular enemies is now expressed in such a way as to be simply a general pronouncing of judgement on those who act against Israel and hence against God.

The hoped-for restoration of the people is accompanied by prayer for the king:

> Let your hand rest on the man of your right hand,
>> on the son of man whom you strengthened for yourself. (80 : 17)

The title 'king' is not used here, but the designation is clear. God upholds his king with his right hand, and it may be that we should understand the picture as that of the king standing at the right-hand side of the deity. The parallel 'son of man' stresses the human nature of the king; he is divinely chosen and an anointed ruler, but he is still a man, with no claims or pretensions beyond this. Stories of the kings—as that of David and Bathsheba in 2 Sam. 11-12—make it clear that the same standards of justice and right conduct were to be expected of them as of ordinary citizens. Royal privilege gives no exemption from responsibility. The status of the king is often indicated by the use of the term 'slave' or 'servant'; he may be described as 'son of your slave-girl' (so for example in 86 : 16). But he is nevertheless the spokesman of his people and divine favour to the king is understood in terms of favour to the whole community.

> We will not turn back from you.
> Revive us and we will invoke your name.
> O God of hosts restore us,
> let your face shine toward us that we may be victorious. (80 : 18-19)

So a climax is reached. Prayer for divine favour is met with the response of loyalty from the people of God. Restoration to life, as from illness or death, will lead to the renewed worship of God, the God who made his secret name known to his people in order that they might address him by name and know that he would respond. The refrain draws together the prayers and the confidence of king and people that the God who has declared himself to them in past experience is the God of present action.

[Other psalms on similar themes, recalling the mighty acts of God are 44, 60, 79, 85, 135, 136.]

The three psalms which have been translated and briefly expounded in this chapter open up various themes: God and the world, God and his people; God as supreme king, God as the controller of world and nations; the nature and problems of human obedience, the experiences of abandonment by God, of distress. We see that they are rarely specific. If they make allusion to a particular moment of Israel's history, this is done in such a way that there is ready movement from the contemplation of that moment to the experiences and needs of other occasions. If they derive from particular kinds of experience—national or personal—it is no longer possible to discover these with certainty. Military language becomes the metaphor for struggle with hostile forces. Description of illness, such as we may detect in the vivid phrases of 22 (see vv. 14-15), are now removed from the particular distress and used as metaphors alongside others (in 22 those of attacking bulls and lions in vv. 12-13, and of bandits and robbers in vv. 16-18). It is when we recognize this that we sense the way in which the words of the psalmists become our own. Their metaphors, drawn out of deep feeling and long use, become ours, often no doubt with a shift in meaning, since we cannot be sure how fully we understand them in every detail. But the poetry reaches out, and awareness of our own position becomes surrounded with the agonies and the assurances of those who over the centuries of Israel's life worshipped with these words and others like them.

One of the effects of using such religious poetry as the vehicle of our own faith and of our own uncertainty is to give us a wider context for where we stand. The uniqueness of our own moment of experience remains, not to be denied. But it is possible to see it now related to typical experiences, to declarations of need and confessions of faith which lift it out of its uniqueness into a larger sphere, where we may both learn from the rich tradition of the psalms and ourselves contribute to their continuing understanding. It is here that we may understand why the psalms came to be known as the 'psalms of David'. Associated with the life of that one particular personage of Israel's past, they come to express the needs and hopes of every worshipper. Seen as showing David's response to changing fortunes and experiences, they come to express the nourishing of religious life in every age.

5

The Nourishing of Religious Life

WE HAVE ALREADY seen that some psalms were provided with titles associating them with particular moments in the life of David; and that there are indications that at certain points in the David stories in the books of Samuel, the intention was that an appropriate psalm should be read as a commentary on the story. In addition, a considerable number of psalms have the words 'for' or 'to' or 'of David' as part of the title. The one preposition used here in Hebrew may have various meanings, and the original meaning of this phrase is very uncertain. In earlier times it was assumed to denote authorship, and similarly other psalms were believed to carry their author's names—Solomon for 72, Moses for 90, and so on. Then it was thought probable that such a phrase indicated a collection, a 'psalter of David' to which some of the psalms had originally belonged, and this view could be supported by the phrase at the end of 72: 'The prayers of David son of Jesse, are ended', which must mark the end of a particular collection. Such a 'psalter of David' need not imply authorship, but simply an association with the temple at Jerusalem, and with the tradition, clearly attested in 1 Chron. 15-16, that David organised temple worship, a tradition which must itself have grown from earlier and more limited ideas. The stories of David as musician and as composer of laments provided a basis for such a development. But a more important element was the fact that David as the first king of the greatest dynasty of Israel's history was also associated with the establishment of Jerusalem as capital city, credited with bringing the Ark there, and hence with its eventual centrality in worship. So 'for David' could be understood to mean 'for the Davidic king'. The recognition that many of the psalms allude to the king, directly or indirectly, and that the king's place in the people's worship must have been vitally important —so, for example Josiah in 2 Kings 22-23—could readily suggest that a Davidic psalter meant one that was largely, perhaps primarily, associated with worship at the temple at Jerusalem, the shrine of the kingdom, and with the functioning of the king as spokesman to God for the people and for God to the people. The detail of this and its extent remain debatable.

These various factors contributed eventually to the view being taken, by both Jews and Christians, that the Psalter was to be associated with David. Psalms are quoted as containing the words of David, speaking as a prophet (so, for example, in Acts 2 : 25-28, 34-35), and speaking therefore words meaningful to much later hearers. A short passage in a psalter from Qumran lists the compositions of David—3,600 psalms, and other songs for particular occasions to make up a total of 4,050 poems: this is clearly a vivid way of saying firmly: 'all psalms must be by David'. The same passage presents him as speaking prophetically. The New Testament writers who claimed this were thus expressing a familiar view of the way in which David's psalms were coming to be understood, and they found here a rich source of illumination for their endeavours at interpreting for themselves and their contemporaries the meaning of Jesus's life and death and resurrection. Such evidence they found in the law, the prophets, and the psalms (Luke 24 : 44).

Such use of the psalms, important as it is to us for understanding how the New Testament writers and their contemporaries worked, has its limitations. It is much more concerned with finding clarification for what is already believed, means of expressing in familiar terms new elements of religious experience, than with letting the psalms speak out of their poetry. Nearer to this was the process by which the psalms were seen in relation to David's life, the experiences of the great king being viewed as typical, as providing patterns for the understanding of the reader's own experience, and as enabling him to see his own needs and uncertainties in a wider context.

The figure of David was particularly appropriate for this. Of course, there were other great personalities of Israel's ancient tradition which were to be similarly important. The words of prophets were re-interpreted along with the appreciation of the agonies of their lives, particularly in the cases of Hosea and Jeremiah. The pattern of faith in the figure of Abraham became a vital element in much later thought, not least that of Paul. But the David tradition was both more extensive and more varied. As we read the stories in the books of Samuel, we have a vivid impression of a real personality, and this in spite of the many uncertainties and historical difficulties which arise. It is the portrait of a great and heroic figure 'warts and all'. Even the later Chronicler, whose portrait of David differs in many respects, does not remove the unsatisfactory sides of David's personality completely, since he includes as a vital part of his narrative David's failure over the census (2 Sam. 24; 1 Chron. 21); and in any case, he assumed that his readers knew the older stories and was inviting them to read those older stories in the light of his own particular emphasis and interpretation.

The figure of David is heroic and tragic; it is marked by loyalty and by treachery; it has moments of glorious self-dedication to God's service and of abysmal failure. He is one who bears the reputation of a just ruler, and yet failed to control or discipline his own sons. He nearly lost his throne to his ambitious son Absalom, and nearly lost it again in the agony of his grief at that son's death. The variety and the contrasts made possible the reading of the psalms against the background of David's life. It was not difficult to interpret particular psalms in relation to particular stories and occasions. Poetic detail, elaborate metaphor, could be unravelled to fit the story as we have it set out in the biblical books, and also the richer tradition which undoubtedly existed side by side with that story.

The relating of psalms to David was to lead on to the relating of them to Christ; and this in its turn too was to bring the position of the individual believer into focus. It is with this in mind that we may now turn to some further psalms, suggesting ways in which their poetry may come to be meaningful to the individual worshipper.

Psalm 24 is complex. It opens (vv. 1-2) with the proclamation of the universal lordship of God and his secure founding of the world. It reaches its climax (vv. 7-10) in the acclamation of the victorious God, acknowledged in his glory and majesty as he comes in triumph to his sanctuary. These themes provide the context for question and answer about the possibility of worship, the problem of the status of man in the very presence of God.

> Who may go up into the mountain of God?
>> Who may stand in his sanctuary?
> The innocent in deed,
>> the cleansed in heart.
> One who has not turned towards false belief,
>> who has not sworn in deceit.
> Such a one will receive blessing from God,
>> triumph from his victorious God.
> Such is the community of those who inquire of him,
>> of those who seek your presence, God of Jacob.
>
> (24 : 3-6)

A fuller and more elaborate statement of this kind appears in 15, where the whole psalm concentrates on the requirements laid upon man. Here, more briefly and with some problems of interpretation, the very centre of man's approach to God is indicated. To be present in the shrine, to stand where it is so clearly proclaimed that God chooses to make his presence known, demands certain basic things. Purity, that is to say, acceptability, is both external and internal: the phrases which open v. 4 refer to both the 'hands', as the members with which a man acts, and the 'heart' or 'mind', that which governs his inner make-up. Ancient Israel was well aware of the propriety of due preparation for worship, and of the degree to which men create a barrier between themselves and God by what they do and are. The phrases which follow may be understood to refer to falsehood, false swearing. But more appropriately we may see here a reference to alien religious practice. The first and basic requirement of Israel's faith was the acknowledgement of God alone: the decalogue begins 'I am your God who brought you out of Egypt, from the house of servitude; you shall not have any other god as rival to me' (Exod. 20 : 2-3). There can be no relationship without the acknowledgement of absolute trust. From this there can come blessing and victory, expressions of the assurance of relationship with God himself, geared to the establishing of well-being and prosperity. The concern of the individual worshipper is taken up into the confidence that the whole community may equally experience this. Those who 'inquire of him', that is desire to know his will and to accept it; those who desire to be in his presence—and again the implication is that no other allegiance is admissible—are, by that desire, recognizable as the people of God.

By setting this searching into the basis of relationship to God in the context of proclamation and acclamation of him, the psalm holds together the awareness of the supremacy of God and the uncertainty in which man must stand. It was with this same instinct that the narrator put together in 2 Sam. 5-6 the theme of David's conquest of Jerusalem and defeat of the Philistines, described in terms of God's protective and victorious power, and that of his bringing the Ark to Jerusalem and of the dangers attaching to that symbol of the holiness of God. It is in the moment of success that we may need to ask most insistently by what right we approach God at all.

Psalm 144 takes the question a little further. Again the context speaks of divine power and help, of confidence in divine victory and deliverance, of assurance at the blessings which God gives in life and well-being (vv. 1-2, 5-8, 9-11, 12-15). But in this the more radical question is asked:

> O God, what is man that you should care for him?
> What is a human being that you should take
>   thought for him?
> Man is like a breath of wind,
>   his days are like a shadow which moves on.
>   (144 : 3-4)

The words echo the similar phrases of 8 : 3-4; there they are answered with affirmation of the glory which God chooses to give to men. They are echoed also in Job 7 : 17-18, where the author gives to them a twist to suggest the relentless and inescapable pressures of God upon man. In 144 the thought expresses both that sense of wonder that God should so concern himself with the created order, and opens up by implication the question so much examined in the book of Job: how can there be a relationship between man in the brevity of his life, the temporary quality of his existence, and God who by definition cannot be so limited. 144 uses a word, here rendered 'breath of wind' (perhaps more familiar from the older translations as 'vanity'), which runs right through the book of Ecclesiastes, that work which most challenges the pretensions of men, describing them all thus.

Psalm 26 sets out the nature of loyalty and obedience.

> Establish my due rights, O God,
>   for I live in an acceptable manner,
>   in God himself I put my trust,
> I shall not falter. (26 : 1)

Security belongs to a life lived in assured confidence in God, but this is not complacency.

> Test me, O God, put me to the test,
>> purify my whole being. (26 : 2)

Confidence lies in acknowledgement of God's loyalty to his worshipper, in the worshipper's repudiation of those who set themselves against his will. With due preparation for worship, the psalmist joins the procession round the altar and so the act of praise at what God has done (vv. 3-7). The affirmation of allegiance continues (v. 8), but it is clear that there is no glib confidence here.

> Do not gather me up with sinners,
>> even with men guilty of bloodshed,
>> in whose hands is impropriety,
> whose right hands are full of bribes. (26 : 9-10)

The psalmist moves to and fro between his expression of allegiance and confidence and his willingness to submit to God's will and his awareness of the precarious nature of his position. So he moves again to affirmation and to appeal, and from this to the acknowledgement of God in public worship.

> I live in an acceptable manner.
>> Redeem me and show me favour.
> My feet stand on even ground,
>> in the assembly of worshippers I bless God.
>>> (26 : 11-12)

The fluctuation of mood is vivid. The range is from confidence and trust to uncertainty and doubt; it is a poignant statement of the experience of God, and of the awareness that it belongs to human nature to move often without cause from hope to despair and from uncertainty to confidence.

Psalm 73 examines more closely the problem of good and evil, of the prosperity of the wicked which appears to cut so sharply across what men understand to be the ways of God in justice. Characteristically the psalm begins with an affirmation:

> How good is God to the upright,
> even God to those acceptable in mind. (73 : 1)

A declaration of the goodness and justice of God provides the setting for the exploration of problems of life and conduct; and this affirmation is echoed in the conclusion of the psalm (vv. 25-28). In fact the Hebrew text of the psalm has a different opening in which we may probably see a later scribe modifying the words to generalise the meaning. By dividing the words differently he could read:

> How good to Israel,
> how good is God to those acceptable in mind.

Thus the insight of the poet who examined his own dilemmas in the context of his confidence in the goodness of God has been lifted to another level. Whatever the problems the individual may face, the assurance of God's enduring benevolence to his people remains unshaken.

The problem is explored in a series of vivid pictures in vv. 3-12; not all of these pictures are entirely clear, but they add up to an eloquent statement of the disregard of God by those who consider that he 'does not care, nor is there any concern with such matters in the Most High' (v. 11). But this is no academic question; it involves the poet's own faith:

> As for me, my feet were almost stumbling,
> my steps were almost brought to slip. (73 : 12)

So he asks whether his endeavours at obedience and purity of life were simply to no purpose (v. 13) as he finds himself plagued all the time, chastened day after day (v. 14). The

81

F

temptation then is to let go, so to stumble that he speaks as do the wicked in disregard of God.

> If I were to say: I will speak as they do,
>   then I should have betrayed the community
>   of your faithful ones. (73 : 15)

To relinquish hold on faith is not for oneself alone: it is the betrayal of that whole community which lives in faith, literally as the children, the sons of God. The answer comes:

> I endeavoured to understand this,
>   but it was a torment to me.
> Until I entered the sanctuary of God,
>   and so came to understand their destiny. (73 : 16-17)

This understanding is expressed again in vivid pictures, suggestive of the separation from God of those who disregard him (vv. 18-20). There is no simple resolving of the problem here, but an awareness that the faith of the community and the experience of standing in the presence of God, offer an assurance of the reality of relationship with him. The bitterness of failure to understand (vv. 21-22) is answered by the assurance of God's presence (vv. 23-24). And with this goes the further affirmation that moves beyond the immediate problem into a confidence which lies beyond direct experience.

> Whom have I in the heavens?
>   Beside you I have no desire on earth.
> If my whole self comes to an end,
>   the rock of my life and my heritage is
>   God himself for ever. (73 : 25-26)

The psalm closes with a contrasting reflection on alienation from God as disaster, and on the prized possession of God as security and refuge (vv. 27-28).

This is a psalm which shows particularly strongly a feature which in fact appears frequently throughout the Psalter. It is reflective. It examines with deep feeling the uncertainties of experience, and the unresolvable problems of human life. Like the author of Job, the poet is able to hold together an intense questioning of the ways of God with a firm grasp of his reality. In the end it is an experience of direct confrontation with God that brings not a solution to the problems but a way of life which is meaningful in itself.

Psalm 109 is one that is often omitted from use because of the violence of its language, and we may appreciate that this poem, like many passages in the Old Testament and no small number in the New, creates difficulties for the reader, especially if it is read or heard without explanation. It is understandable that it should be little used in worship, but the expurgating of the biblical text to remove all that is uncongenial has the disadvantage that we are then less able to appreciate the range of biblical thought and so the less likely to gain full insight into the claims it makes. While it is clearly improper to treat the biblical writings as if they were to be kept separate from other religious works of the Christian and Jewish traditions, it is equally unsatisfactory merely to pick and choose what appeals to us. By such a process we deprive ourselves of the fuller context of those passages which evoke an immediate response. To say this is not to suggest that such a psalm as this is free of gross misunderstandings of the nature of God. But to appreciate the poet's mind, we must try to understand where he stands and why he speaks as he does.

There is sharp contrast here between the castigation of the wicked, the opponents of the psalmist, upon whom the most terrible judgement is invoked in the first part of the psalm (vv. 1-20), and the assurance of God's consistent and unfailing care which is affirmed in the second part (vv. 21-31). The emphasis of this second part is brought out most clearly in such words as these:

> Help me, O my God,
>> deliver me in accordance with your loyalty.
> So they (the opponents) may know that this is your
>> hand,
>> it is you yourself who have done this.
> If they curse,
>> then you bless.
> May my opponents be put to shame,
>> but let your servant rejoice. (109 : 26-28)

The overthrow of the wicked is the concern of God; the deliverance of the worshipper, whether individual or king as spokesman for the people, will itself demonstrate to them the sole action of God. It is evident that the realm of thought in which the poet operates is that of concern about those who set themselves against God; they are his enemies because they are God's enemies. The highly poetic statements of doom for them are to be understood particularly in this context.

At the same time, we may recognize that the intensity and violence of the language witnesses to a deep-seated agony at what the poet feels. This language is not to be understood at the purely literal level of malice and vituperation against particular personal opponents, still less narrowed by application to particular enemies of individual or party or nation. It belongs to the deep concern which the poet feels at the disorder of human life. What is here expressed in terms of utmost hostility towards those who frustrate or seek to frustrate the will of God, is of a piece with the bitterness of speech which the author of the book of Job uses to express the agony of his concern at the evident disorder of human experience. The author of Job indeed goes further in that he finds himself forced into the position of making accusations against God himself for the injustice of the world. If, as is reasonable, we do not care for the direct onslaughts of the psalmist—

May his days be few,
   what is under his care be taken by another.
May his sons be orphans,
   his wife a widow.
May his sons be entirely without home,
   let them beg, beseech from their ruins. (109 : 8-10)

—we must recognize that protest at what is wrong is here being expressed in the harshest possible terms. This is no mealy-mouthed moralising comment; it is acute agony at the state of the world. The metaphors derive from the actualities of human bitterness; they have been taken over to express a deep concern at the disorder of man's life as it is experienced.

There is no question of giving a merely literal interpretation to such language, for this would do less than justice to the breadth of the poet's concern. Nor is it appropriate to dismiss such sentiments as improper, sub-Christian; they derive from a life-setting which was violent and harsh. They are no more violent than the saying attributed to Jesus, calling for judgement: 'it would be better for him if a great millstone were hung round his neck and he were thrown into the sea' (Mark 9 : 42), a saying which is to be measured in terms of protest against evil rather than in terms of literal fulfilment. Perhaps, even if we find such poetry as 109 unacceptable— and there is much of this kind in the Psalter, whole psalms and single verses —we should respect the emotional heat which calls forth such protest, and see it as a witness to the intensity of the struggle against evil and oppression and dehumanisation which all too often become for us too familiar for more than passing interest. We may recall too that David, in the white heat of indignation at the conduct of the rich man in Nathan's parable (2 Sam. 12), pronounced his belief that such a man must be regarded as belonging to the realm of death— only to discover that his anger must be directed against himself for his own betrayal of the standards of right which a king must uphold.

Psalm 101 expresses just that standard of justice. No direct clue is to be found here of the psalm's original setting, but its final verse strongly suggests that it is a statement of the king's responsibility as judge of his people and as upholder of right:

> Every day I will silence
> all the wicked in the land;
> I will cut off from the city of God
> all who do evil. (101 : 8)

The psalm is in effect a confession of adherence to a right standard, an act of praise for God whose justice the king upholds.

> Loyalty and justice I sing,
> to you, O God, I pronounce a psalm. (101 : 1)

The main body of the poem sets out aspects of right conduct, indications of what must be maintained. If in origin it is an acknowledgement by the king of his duties as upholder of right, it becomes a basis for examination by the worshipper of his own adherence to such a standard.

Psalm 54 is one that has a title linking it with a particular incident of David's life: 'when the people of Ziph came and told Saul: David is in fact in hiding with us,' an incident related in 1 Sam. 23 : 14-19 as part of the story of Saul's pursuit of David. Much of that story turns on the interplay between treachery to David and loyalty to him, and on the tension between the prospect of Saul's narrowly failing to catch David and the divine protection of David, the chosen king. The linking of the psalm in this way narrows its meaning, but illustrates these wider concerns.

> O God, give me victory in the power of your name,
> by your great might establish my right.
> O God, hear my prayer,
> listen to the words which I speak.
> Aliens have risen against me,
> tyrants seek my life,
> they do not consider God. (54 : 1-3)

86

It is evident that these opening verses are of a very general character, applicable to any situation of distress and need. The words of v. 3 suggest a picture of one who feels himself isolated, confronted by a hostile world which pays no heed to God's will. Such isolation is a commonly felt experience; it is vividly expressed in the portrayal of Jeremiah's agony of loneliness (cf. e.g. Jer. 15 : 10) and presented likewise in the desertion of Jesus by his disciples.

In contrast to such isolation, the poet affirms the presence of God.

> But God is my helper,
>> my lord the chief support of my life.
> Let their evil recoil on those who watch me,
>> silence them with your truth. (54 : 4-5)

It is confidence in God as sole support, the assurance that the forces hostile to the poet, and hence understood as hostile to God, will be subdued.

> Willingly I shall offer sacrifice,
>> I shall praise your name, O God, because it is good.
> For from all adversity you have delivered me,
>> I look in triumph at my enemies. (54 : 6-7)

The experience of release, the restoration of the poet from that which threatened his mind, is expressed in the offering of worship—a sacrifice beyond that which is legally required, the utterance of the formula of praise so often to be found in the imperative form: Praise the name of God, for it is good (cf. e.g. the refrains in 136).

The linking of this psalm to a particular David narrative shows the freedom with which the words of the psalm are interpreted, since evidently they are not concerned with that kind of rivalry which is depicted in the stories of Saul and David. It also shows how those stories are themselves being read not at the level of accounts of the ancient past, but as

87

symbols of present needs. They are losing their particular reference and being themselves generalised into parables of human experience. Psalm and story are together being re-interpreted into relationship with the needs of other generations.

Psalm 137 provides another example of such generalisation, here from the deep anguish of exile in Babylonia in the sixth century B.C. The psalm is unique in its precise reference to the experience of those years, though there are many indications in the Psalter that deliverance from exile, the gathering to Jerusalem of the scattered people, became a focal point for much of the hope of the later Jewish community (so e.g. 106 : 47). Here there is a more complex reflection on what exile means. The opening verses concentrate on the agony:

> Beside the rivers of Babylon,
>   there we sat, yes wept,
>   at our remembering of Zion.
> Upon the willow-trees in that land,
>   we hung our lyres.
> For there they asked of us,
>   our captors asked the words of a song,
>   those who made us lament asked for joy:
> 'Sing for us
>   a song of Zion'.
> How could we sing
>   the song of God,
>   in a foreign land? (137 : 1-4)

The poet looks back to the moment of exile and relives the experience. Vividly he pictures the captives in an alien land. Distress at the loss of the temple, focus of religious feeling and longing, evokes lament. The symbol of the hanging up of the lyres is not fully clear; it suggests that the instruments are dumb, reduced to silence and sharing in their owners' desolation. Contrast is drawn with the imaginative portrayal

88

of the captors' demands. The rendering 'those who made us lament' is uncertain, but it sets the demand for joy against the imposition of lament. The poignancy of the last phrases suggests the sense of alienation, of loss of centre, of the hopes concentrated on Jerusalem as the place associated with God's enduring contact with his people.

The picture thus drawn evokes the sentiments which attach to Jerusalem, and it is with this in mind that the poet moves to a new moment:

> If I forget you, Jerusalem,
>   let my right hand wither.
> Let my tongue cling to the roof of my mouth,
>   if I do not remember you;
> if I do not set up Jerusalem
>   above my chief joy. (137 : 5-6)

Here is the centre of the poem, concentrated on Jerusalem and its meaning to the worshipper. Much of biblical psalmody focuses here, for in the later stages of the biblical period the Psalter is limited entirely to the one holy place in Jerusalem. Affection for the shrine (122), recall of its special position (87), delineation of its divine choice (78), are all frequent themes. Love of Jerusalem, both as city and as holy place, forms a theme often closely linked with that of the Davidic king, as, for example, in 127, traditionally associated with Solomon and developing the theme that God is the true builder of his shrine and guardian of his city (vv. 1-2), and the theme of sons, the line of rulers of the Davidic dynasty (vv. 3-7). This combination of themes, very fully developed in 2 Sam. 7, forms a central element in the continuity of Old Testament religious thought. 137 presents the theme of Jerusalem in a solemn declaration, invoking disaster upon the worshipper who should forget that holy place.

The counterpart to this declaration of allegiance to Jerusalem lies in the invocation of judgement upon the enemies of Zion.

> Remember, O God,
>   for the people of Edom,
>   the day of Jerusalem;
> they who said: Lay it completely bare,
>   even to its very foundations.
> O people of Babylon the destroyer,
>   blessings for the one who requites you
>   for what you did to us.
> Blessings for the one who seizes, who smashes,
>   your children upon a rock. (137 : 7-9)

One aspect of this terrible call for doom is the horrific nature of warfare, ancient and modern. But more important for our understanding is the recognition that we are dealing in reality less with historical themes than with those themes transposed into symbols of hostile forces, the enemies of God. Many Old Testament passages, particularly in the prophetic books (so e.g. Isa. 34; Ezek. 34; Obadiah), elaborate on the theme of judgement on Edom, itself in part derived from the ancient tradition of the rivalry of Jacob and Esau as figures representing the two peoples of Israel and Edom. That historic conflicts contributed to the theme is likely. But Edom becomes one of the chief symbols for the alien, hostile world. And Babylon, conqueror of Judah and destroyer of Jerusalem, becomes just such another, eventually to be used as a conventional term for whatever hostile power oppressed the Jewish people—as for example in the book of Daniel reflecting the harsh conflicts of the Maccabean struggles of the second century B.C., or the pressures of Roman authority on the early Christian community as depicted in vivid symbol by the book of the Revelation in the New Testament. It is again an invocation of longing for the overthrow of all that is directed against the will of God, the conviction that in the end that will must triumph, even through the failure of the people of God, and the judgements passed upon them and interpreted in terms of conquest and exile. The future lies through the victory which God brings out of defeat. The New

Testament writers transposed that victory in defeat out of the experiences of Israel into the interpretation of the cross.

It was Coleridge who said: 'Poetry gives most pleasure when only generally and not perfectly understood'. P. J. Cavanagh, in a broadcast talk, commented: 'At first, that's startling; it seems to offer a cloak for every posturing loon in love with the sound of his own voice. But, after a moment's thought, we know that it is perfectly true. We have all been moved, pleased, intrigued by groups of words we did not wholly understand at first—or even at last. That is, we didn't understand them with that part of our minds we call our understanding, yet we seemed to understand them in some other way' (*The Listener*, 23 June 1977).

As true also of the psalms, as poetry, as it is of the rich and allusive language of the liturgy. Of course, this is no excuse either for not making the best endeavour to understand what is meant or for mere mystification and slipshod interpretation. It is the recognition that the psalms can speak directly from poet to reader, to illuminate the nature of belief, to enlarge the understanding of God, to deepen the apprehension of the world and of human experience. Such poetry and such willingness to hear what it has to say to us may open 'doors of perception' for us to the further and less accessible reaches of religious life and thought.

Translations of the Psalms

MOST OF THE translations of the biblical text in this book are my own. This is not because I claim any superiority for them, but because in many instances I have attempted by a particular rendering to bring out the point immediately at issue. I have exercised some freedom in translating, not least in using the word 'God' (as is done by Peter Levi) rather than attempting to find an equivalent for the divine personal name, transliterated YHWH and often, though uncertainly, vocalised Yahweh, and equally often rendered with the conventionally capitalised form LORD. Inevitably the avoidance of this and others of the various terms and titles for the deity used in the psalms has necessitated paraphrase at some points.

The number and variety of translations of the psalms is such that only brief and incomplete notes can be given here. But the fundamental point is unaffected. The reader should choose that version which most appeals at a given moment and use it with the recognition that no translation is perfect, that our knowledge of the ancient text and of the Hebrew language gradually changes so that older translations inevitably lack the influence of this more recent knowledge. But since the translation of poetry is more than mere rendering into equivalent terms, the value of a particular version may rest in its quality of poetry, even where details must be recognized to be erroneous. For many, the *Coverdale* translation of the *Book of Common Prayer*, will, for its familiarity and its quality as poetry, remain the best loved. Its more modern form, the *Revised Prayer Book Psalter*, improves it by removing obvious error, though not always preserving its poetic flavour. The versions in the *Authorised (King James')
Version* and the updated forms of the *Revised Version* and the *Revised Standard Version* have varying degrees of reli-

ability and datedness. The same must be said of the most
modern translations: the *New English Bible,* often good but
with too many vagaries. The *New American Bible* and the
Jerusalem Bible both stem from Roman Catholic circles; the
latter has a flavour which derives from its French literary
background; it is also published in an edition arranged for
reading and recitation. The *Gelineau* psalter, attractive for
corporate use, though too much geared to rather artificial
poetic structures; the *Good News Bible* (*Today's English
Version*) readable and simple; the *Living Bible,* curiously
rendering the psalms as prose, and offering too much a paraphrase rather than translation; the *Modern Language Bible,*
a straightforward, conventional rendering. Particular mention
may be made of the *Knox* translation, also Roman Catholic,
which attempts, with varying success, a degree of literalness
of rendering that may help to bring the reader close to the
meaning of the original, though the text is poorly set out as
prose. The recent translation by *Peter Levi,* published by
Penguin Books, does not always succeed as poetry, but has
a simplicity which is often attractive. It also has a very clear
introduction by Nicholas de Langhe. A number of modern
translations provide titles for each psalm, specifying their
content; the limitations of such titles have been noted above
(p. 52).

Over a period of time, the reader may find it useful to
compare different translations, recognizing that in the psalms
as in other parts of the Bible, such different renderings may
in themselves provide partial commentaries. They represent
particular ways of understanding the text, of handling the
problems of what appear to be textual errors, and by their
use of variant manuscripts and ancient versions (often though
not always indicated in marginal notes to the translations)
indicate something of the wealth of material available for the
attempt at recovering both what may be considered the best
text in any given instance and, more importantly, some of the
stages through which the text has gone and the differing
levels of its interpretation.

Suggestions for Further Reading

Commentaries: For stimulus, U. E. Simon, *Psalms* (Mowbrays Mini-commentary, 1970). As good working commentaries, J. W. Rogerson and J. McKay, *The Psalms,* 3 vols (Cambridge Bible Commentary, 1977—based on N.E.B.); A. A. Anderson, *The Psalms,* 2 vols (New Century Bible, Oliphants, 1972); J. H. Eaton, *The Psalms* (Torch Bible Commentary SCM Press, 1967).

General books on the Psalms: H. Ringgren, *The Faith of the Psalmists* (SCM Press, 1963); C. F. Barth, *Introduction to the Psalms* (Blackwell, 1966, translated by R. A. Wilson); J. H. Eaton, *Kingship and the Psalms* (SCM Press, 1976); J. H. Hayes, *Understanding the Psalms* (Judson Press, Valley Forge, 1976).

Reference to the wider range of literature may be found in the general introductions to the Old Testament and in the various one-volume commentaries.

The reader's attention is also drawn to the Liturgical Psalter published in 1980 in *The Alternative Service Book*. An earlier sample form appeared as *Twenty-five Psalms from a Modern Liturgical Psalter* by D. L. Frost and A. A. Macintosh (Church Information Office, 1973) and the whole Psalter as *The Psalms —a new translation for Worship* (Collins, 1977). It is generally simple and effective, though tied too closely to the particular 'chanting' system assumed. But it provides a good modern alternative to the Coverdale rendering.

Acknowledgements

Acknowledgements are due to the following:

G. Vermes, *The Dead Sea Scrolls in English*. Penguin Books Ltd., Harmondsworth, Middlesex, p. 175, for the quotation on p. 28.

P. J. Cavanagh, 'Guessworks', *The Listener*, 23 June 1977, p. 810, for the quotation on p. 91.